T0148216

"Dearest Angel..."

"*Dearest Angel...*"

[A Father's Post-Abortion Journal of Hurt and Healing]

William D. Zimmerman

iUniverse, Inc.
New York   Bloomington

"Dearest Angel..."
A Father's Post-Abortion Journal of Hurt and Healing

Copyright © 2010 by William D. Zimmerman

All rights reserved. No part of this book may be used or reproduced by any means, graphic, electronic, or mechanical, including photocopying, recording, taping or by any information storage retrieval system without the written permission of the publisher except in the case of brief quotations embodied in critical articles and reviews.

iUniverse books may be ordered through booksellers or by contacting:

iUniverse
1663 Liberty Drive
Bloomington, IN 47403
www.iuniverse.com
1-800-Authors (1-800-288-4677)

Because of the dynamic nature of the Internet, any Web addresses or links contained in this book may have changed since publication and may no longer be valid. The views expressed in this work are solely those of the author and do not necessarily reflect the views of the publisher, and the publisher hereby disclaims any responsibility for them.

ISBN: 978-1-4502-3140-4 (sc)
ISBN: 978-1-4502-3141-1 (ebook)
ISBN: 978-1-4502-3142-8 (dj)

Printed in the United States of America

iUniverse rev. date: 6/22/2010

Dedication

This book is dedicated to the following:

My reasons for living; Christy, Ian, Hunter, Seth and James
My mother and father; Rita and Doug

This labor of love is also dedicated to the voices of men who
feel alone in their grief. You are *never* alone.

Most of all, this book and all of the countless number of
hours I've worked on it are dedicated to the angel who
inspired it all.

WDZ.

Acknowlegements

I would like to acknowledge and thank the authors mentioned in the Recommended Reading section for their work and for helping my project with direction and inspiration.

Additionally, I would also like to thank the authors & publishers who've allowed me to reprint portions of their work; Tom Golden, Seal Press and Family Relations Journal.

I would also like to extend a thank you to the musicians in the Recommended Listening Section for helping me maintain my sanity.

Special thanks to Johnny Indovina of Human Drama/Sound of the Blue Heart for the permission to quote you and reprint your lyrics. Also, thanks for the phone call and for playing "I Keep a Close Watch" for "the guy who drove up from St. Louis."

To Mike & Tara of Lycia and Ronan of VNV Nation for the permission to reprint your words. To Conrad of Stay Frightened for the same and for keeping me laughing. To Stephanie for keeping Conrad laughing. Thank you all.

Extra Special mention to Claus Larsen of Leaether Strip for the permission to reprint your words. More than that, though, for your volume of work which has served as inspiration to me not only musically and lyrically, but also personally. Also, thanks for not getting mad when I called 15 years ago. It's a privilege to call you a friend and to be called a friend by you. And, to Kurt for keeping my friend inspired and alive during his dark days, thank you as well.

More thanks.........

To my best friend ("brother" is perhaps more suitable) Mick V., for all the late night steak dinners, concerts, beers and trips back in time – for the endless laughs, occasional tears and far more memories than I can count - thanks is never enough. Here's a "fanatical dance" and a "conundrum" for you.

To Denise for not "dragging me kicking and screaming" since I actually published this book.

To Kurt from GuysForLife for your words of encouragement as well as your friendship.

To my old friend Nikki C., for all the phone conversations and for buying my Prince CDs so many years ago.

To Donnie & Ken for the privilege of sharing the stage with you, also Kate, Shannon and Dustin: all of you most importantly for the true friends that you always have been.

To Jeff (R.I.P.) for all that you stood for, for the privilege of recording with you and for your time here on earth.

To the Baha'i community of the Metro-East area.

To my editorial staff for helping to fine tune this book.

To Dr. Heather Brice of SLU, Dr. Dennis Norem, Charlie Stocker, Dr. Warren Fournier II and Tim Jenkins.

To Pam Decoteau at the Art History Dept. of SIU-Edwardsville, for your classes that taught me to look at the world differently.

To the other teachers who made a difference for me; Gary Swalley, Peg Spellman & Marion Thompson.

To Jane and Marilyn for direction.

To Pam Richards for your light and guidance.

To Sarah for the jpg. angel.

To Christopher and Amy Savoie for your communication and inspiring story.

To Chris Rini, Ashleigh Wiens, Shawn Waggener, the London team (for your hard work) and everyone at IUniverse for the outstanding support and service.

To my mother and father for instilling values in me that got me through the rough times.

To the Zimmerman, Hackett, Drueke, Glover and Hill Families.

To the boys for making waking up in the morning that much more worthwhile, for your humor and your imagination.

To Christy, for all of your unconditional love and support, for your curiosity, tolerance and patience as I documented these demons of my past, as I edited and obsessively re-edited, for bringing me back to earth on days when I wanted to pull my hair out with this book, or scrap it altogether, for your respect, for believing in me when I doubt myself....most of all for being along for the ride. Without you I'd be lost.

Contents

"In my heart there is a vigil,
And these eyes but close to look within; and yet I live,
But grief should be the instructor of the wise; Sorrow is
knowledge; they who know the most must mourn the deepest.

I have done men good, and I have met with good
even among men.
Since that all nameless hour
Now to my task........."

- Lord Byron

10th Anniversary Prayer

Dearest One,

Some call You God. Others call You Allah. However, as we know, labels are basically for convenience even though they are somewhat necessary.

It's often been said that what doesn't kill us only makes us stronger. Someone needs to rephrase that.

It's not solely the "what" or the "situation."

How about, "What doesn't kill us only makes us stronger as long as we have faith and firm ground?"

Without taking off our socks and walking over the coals of Hell, we can't really begin to know or appreciate the pastures of Heaven.

As this story reads, You know I've been to both.

You were there the whole time. It was most significantly because of You that I made it through alive. I believe that You were also there with her, whether she wanted to believe that or not.

You were the light that came into my room when all I cared to feel was dark. You were the ground beneath my feet when I walked on a cold cement floor or made tracks in the snow.

You were the one patting me on my back, the one who wouldn't let me quit when I wanted to scrap this book. It was You who held the greater purpose of this project and wouldn't allow me to quit life.

You were and have always been the perfect combination of words I strived to write down. You were also the perfect picture that I tried so hard to put into a frame. You were in the eyes of the children who stared back at me.

While it's often said that You are the Remover of Difficulties, isn't it more fitting to say that You are the Guidance through Difficulties?

It was You who blessed me with wonderful friends and family. I am grateful to You for the blessings as well as the challenges during the course of the past ten years.

I hope and trust that your inspiration has graced the words herein.

So I am closing this chapter of my life and I am giving this book back to You. I'm placing it in your hands, now. Only You can take this and make it as effective as possible in the lives of even just a few people (but hopefully more).

May this book provide even one tiny part of the re-affirmation or the restoration of faith, family and foundation in someone's life.

Always,
WDZ 01/02/2009

I

Foreword

Every writer or painter has reasons for the colors of paint or the words they choose. Behind every tragedy lies a reason for growth and hope. Often tragedy inspires art and therefore, the two are often intertwined. The words on a page or drops of paint on a canvas are like the blood of the soul of the artistic. In the film *Dead Poets Society*, Robin Williams's character, Mr. Keating said: "Medicine, law, business, and engineering - these are noble pursuits and necessary to sustain life. But poetry, beauty, romance, love…these are what we stay alive for."

Moreover, I don't believe in coincidence. I believe in purpose.

** ** **

I have been blessed with many gifts in my life: a wonderful family, several very close friends and the resources to bring my art to life. It's only been in recent years that I have realized that such precious gifts should never be taken for granted.

I have occasionally asked myself the question, "Why acknowledge all of the gifts that I've been blessed with and not put them to good use?" Likewise, as an artist, I've asked myself the question, "Why not share the moments that I've experienced regardless of whether or not they were filled with joy or sadness?" Even if some of my experiences contained within this book are somewhat frightening or depressing, if they are noteworthy enough, couldn't someone possibly gain a positive new perspective after reading about them?

Perhaps there's someone I've never met who lives in a place that I've never traveled to who might gain a new perspective by reading about the experiences that I have written down. Maybe there are people out there who might feel less uncomfortable and alone after realizing that others have shared similar highs and lows, loves and losses. I have seen reactions from people who have listened to my music and from those who have read

3

examples of my writing. I've also been fortunate enough to see the gratitude in the faces of artists who've inspired me and to whom I have expressed appreciation.

There have been a countless amount of wonderful articles and books regarding abortion recovery written by or for women. Not nearly as many have been written by men or for men who have suffered from the loss of their children being aborted. Unfortunately, silent and few are the voices of the men who have been equally responsible for the creation of a life and subsequently scarred by the loss of their child. That's partly why you are reading what you are reading now.

Having surveyed the last several years of my life, I cannot help but acknowledge that there are indeed a number of purposes in writing this book. What drove me to endure the lonely late nights when my pen couldn't write as fast as the bullet train of thoughts that rushed through the snow storm inside my mind? What kept me going when I decided to write after times when this project sat on the shelf for weeks or months?

** ** **

HOW DID IT ALL BEGIN?

This book began approximately one year and six months after my 25th birthday - around the summer of 2000. I began writing this material as a way of purging emotions after encountering and enduring a tragedy that I had never imagined I would have to go through. That tragic situation was the abortion of my child. Nothing could prepare me for the devastating experience of losing a child and the emotions I would encounter in the aftermath. The many thoughts and emotions that I was experiencing after the abortion were becoming far too much for my mind to contain. There was only one thing that I knew I could do as a way to survive mentally and emotionally and perhaps make some sense of the growing chaos inside of me. That was to write.

Around June or July of 2000, I determined that I needed a format to document and organize these thoughts and feelings I had. A journal was the easiest way that I knew of to do that. Also, a journal is a wonderful tool for dispensing the "brutal truth" and raw emotion. A journal won't lie or mislead nor will it say something different the next time you seek its counsel. Similar to the word "journal" itself is the word "journey." As I've found, these two words share special significance for me. The action of putting pen to paper is similar to turning the key in the ignition of your car. You may not always be sure where the ride or "journey" is going to take you. You just know that each word written is another step on the gas pedal or another turn off the highway. Depending on the flow of traffic, weather and road construction or conditions otherwise unknown in advance, a journal might not take you to the exact locations you had expected or at the exact speed you had planned. However, it could lead you to locations that might surprise and enlighten you.

This project really began as a desperate cry for help. Essentially, I was initially crying out to myself in an effort to find some sort of organization or vehicle for therapy after experiencing the abortion of my own child. A storm of thoughts and emotions had been slowly building up during the course of eighteen months. The cracks in the walls of my soul were beginning to appear like the different colored road lines on a road map.

The journal started with what became the "Letters" section. My initial reaction was to tell our child what I was thinking and feeling through writing letters. This really seemed to be the easiest way to do this. Sometimes I signed the letters "Daddy," sometimes "Me," and sometimes I left them unsigned. Maybe that was dependant upon how close or how distant I was feeling to our child on those particular days. The original working title for this project was "Dearest Angel: Letters to the Angel I Lost to Abortion." However, I felt that title to be too limiting. I feel the current title is more fitting.

The interesting thing about the letters though, is the fact that they are written herein almost exactly as I wrote them all those years ago. When I started writing the letters, the last things that concerned me were punctuation, grammar and sentence fragments. My primary concerns were to document thoughts and basically pour my heart out to my angel. Other than the occasional spelling correction, the letters appear pretty much as they were written in that worn out, old blue three-subject notebook that I started this project with. Soon after the Letters section started so did the section which would become The Story.

During the composition of the passages which would comprise the Story section, I spent a seemingly countless amount of hours painstakingly recalling as many memories and details as I could. I mentally retraced the trips to Kansas and back home again. I relived the lonely nights and retraced the footprints in the snow.........over and over again. Eventually, I decided to include the Foreword and when life came full circle, I was able to complete the Afterword.

During the first months of writing the Letters and pieces of the Story section, I realized that there were perhaps far more boxes of memories inside of me than I had previously imagined; boxes that needed to be dusted off and their contents organized. In fact, that didn't take very long to realize. As it was so often the case, I would grab the blue notebook I was writing in or sit at my sticker-covered keyboard and start writing whatever words or musical notes came out of me. The first paragraphs of the Story section were very raw as were the letters. A few times writing was like lighting candles and occasionally peeking up to see the streams of wax that have melted on the side of the trays and taking in the candles' different smells. However, writing was more often like taking a single key and unlocking the floodgates, allowing a seemingly uncontrollable force of water to rush from my mind and onto the paper.

Soon I realized that I might have enough material to write a large enough volume of thoughts to call a "book." It also occurred to me early on in this writing that a work of this nature- that is, a documentation of the male's experience of abortion might have a potential reading audience. So, somewhere along the line I realized the possibility that one of my main questions might eventually have an answer. That question was, "What *was* the greater purpose of this abortion in relation to my life?" The answer, of course is that potentially, someone else could benefit from reading about my experiences.

** ** **

WHAT THIS BOOK IS

First and foremost, this book is a tribute to the baby, or as I prefer to say, my "angel," whom I lost to abortion. This is also a tribute to every man who has ever lost a child to abortion and has felt the emotional Hell during the months or even years that followed.

Additionally, every time I sit down at the computer or grab a pen and notebook, I feel like I'm writing the obituary, delivering the eulogy and organizing the wake and the funeral for the child who never received a proper memorial service. I also like to think of this book as the celebration of life that commonly comes after the funeral when the family unites, usually at a family member's house.

This book is a documentation of my struggle and growth. It represents my efforts to take what I could from a negative situation and turn it into a positive experience for myself and hopefully, others.

You are going to read about many good times and bad times. You are also going to read a lot about my guilt and regret-two of the many demons that I became very much acquainted with.

I'll tell you about my love/hate relationship with *memory*; the sometimes grueling experience of recalling moments in time as though they occurred only yesterday. I'm also going to tell you of moments, hours, days or even months that were at times, agonizing and sometimes severely depressing for me. I'll even carry you through moments when I questioned whether or not I wanted to wake up the next morning.

There are, however, also snapshots of happiness and some scenes that might bring a smile to your face while reading this book. In any case, these are all moments of a human experience and I'm ashamed of none of them. Furthermore, if you find yourself experiencing similar thoughts and feelings as I did, you should not be ashamed either.

This is a document of sadness and happiness, of despair and hope, of emptiness and fulfillment and of suffering and healing.

** ** **

WHAT THIS BOOK IS NOT

This book is NOT, in any way, an intention to take a stance on the issue of abortion itself. This book is not Pro-Life nor is it Pro-Choice. I view it as Pro-Human and Pro-Healing. In other words, the purpose of my writing is not to preach whether or not I think abortion is right or wrong nor is it to challenge those individuals who've had honest and valid feelings on either side of the issue. Whether you are pro-life or pro-choice, you likely have very strong feelings regarding the topic of abortion-feelings that are very honest and *human*.

It is not my intention, in any shape or form, to criticize my ex-girlfriend's name or reputation. In fact, I have taken great care to protect her privacy. I have removed the names of the towns we lived in. I have also changed her name in this book out of respect for her. At the same time, all elements within this book are blunt honesty as I know it. Furthermore, this book does not seek to compare my experiences to those of my ex-girlfriend.

This book is also not a statement regarding the stage at which life begins. The value of life should not be dependant upon the stage of development of an unborn child. Neither should the values of the hopes and dreams that go along with that loss.

My intent is to capture the honest and human experience of abortion, bereavement and post-abortion trauma from one man's perspective. It's really as simple as that.

I'm not a celebrity nor am I a professor of health, psychology or biology. I'm not a self-help guru either. I'm not more important nor am I less important than the next person. Simply put, I am a human being who is sharing a story.

I didn't want this book to be a clinical How-To or Step-by-Step manual. I hope that you find this book to be similar to either a personal conversation with me or an invitation to peek inside one of my journals.

What I care about is this: the idea that someone I've never met who lives in a place I've never traveled to could possibly be helped by my experiences or at least feel not quite as alone or ashamed.

** ** **

ON MEMORY

Memory can often be a blessing. A glance through old photographs might remind you of the time when you took your girlfriend to that concert on your first date. Memory can also remind you of the park your mom or dad took you to nearly every other weekend during your childhood.

However, while memory can be a blessing, it can just as often be a curse. One of my favorite songwriters, Johnny Indovina of the bands Human Drama & Sound of the Blue Heart said the following words regarding the topic of *Memory:* "I think it's one of the most deadly things. The simple act of recalling something puts that hole right back in your stomach as you felt when whatever event happened, happened."

Memory allows the most painful moments in life to be relived over and over again. You never forget where you were and how you felt when you split up with your first girlfriend or boyfriend. You most likely never forgot where you were and what you were doing when the terrorist attacks on September 11, 2001 occurred. I know I didn't forget. I was sitting at my desk at work and I was wearing a white shirt that day.

It would be fair to label memory as a curse when it becomes painful to "put those holes right back into your heart." However, even in that case, at least one positive element can be said about memory. Memory can possibly allow us the opportunity for mental and spiritual growth. While the proverbial "light at the end of the tunnel" can often be dimmed, positive opportunities can still manifest themselves; opportunities for personal progress and even perhaps the opportunities to help another person. It really just becomes a matter of where and when.

Memory can be instrumental in constructing new patterns of growth provided that we learn from our mistakes and misfortunes and outgrow our comfort zones. So, it can be fair to say that memory can be a blessing as well as a blessing in disguise. It most certainly has been both for me.

I had to walk again through dimly lit hallways and crawl once again through the pitch black corners of memories of the past ten years. I had to fight the cobwebs and dust off some old boxes to locate some things I wanted, other things I didn't and some things I just plain needed.

So, as I brush off the dust and dig up the past ten years,
I give you.........
All of the memories
All of the hurt
All of the anger
All of the depression
All of the regret

I also give you.......
All of the healing
And all of the hope

II

The Story

** ** **

"Instead of misery loves company,
misery breeds empathy."
- Amy Savoie

** ** **

"Sometimes our fate resembles a fruit tree in winter. Who would think that those branches would turn green again and blossom, but we hope it, we know it."

- Johann Wolfgang von Goethe

TREE OF LIFE

A Christmas tree sticker torn in two parts remains in the lower right-hand corner of the rear-view mirror in my gray Ford Ranger pickup truck. Her father gave it to me at the Christmas party in 1998 during one of my visits to see her. I have kept that sticker on my rear-view mirror for a reason. It's a reminder; a reminder to learn from the past as I look through the windshield toward the blessings as well as the challenges that exist on the road ahead of me.

A common symbol of life is that of a tree. Often, terms used to illustrate existence and connectedness are "tree of life," "family tree," or even "roots." The sticker in my rear-view mirror was split into two, though not intentionally. It's sort of symbolic, really. Much like the separation I felt from the loss of our child to abortion and the end of my relationship with the mother, so were the branches of our "tree of life" torn in half.

As the sticker can be seen as a symbol, so can the mirror. In a way, it's much like memory. The mirror is a bit smudgy with fingerprints-stained by the actions of the past or "rear view." While memory may be a bit cloudy at times, we can usually get better visual images when we look at life in that rear-view mirror of memory. I think that most often we don't realize the effects of some situations until we've achieved a safe distance from them and have allowed those situations to pass. It's much easier to view the past than it is to be conscious of everything that is shaping our lives in the present time. I once heard someone say, "Hindsight is 20/20" or perfect vision. Whoever said that was correct.

I look past the sticker in the rear-view mirror, past the smudgy fingerprints to the past several years of my life and survey the panorama of events and emotions that have shaped the person that I am today.

** ** **

MEETING

We met in an internet chat room during the later part of autumn in 1998. This particular chat room was a part of an online community where people who were into the "Goth" subculture would gather to chat, post blogs or engage in discussions in a variety of forums. For several months I knew her only by her screen name. Out of respect for her privacy, I will not reveal her real name. I will refer to her in this book only by the name, "Anne."

During the course of a few months prior to our first meeting, Anne and I occasionally chatted online and spoke a few times on the telephone. We developed a close friendship fairly quickly.

It was mid November of 1998 when I agreed to visit Anne in Kansas. It was there that she was attending college at the time. The drive to Kansas was approximately five hours from Illinois; where I was living. Under normal circumstances, the trip is very boring especially when country music and the occasional livestock report are the only things on the radio stations outside of St. Louis and Kansas City. It didn't help that I had a marginally working cassette deck that produced just about as much static as it did music.

However, I remember the feeling of looking forward to our first meeting, the anticipation. In retrospect, I think one of the things that I learned around this time was this: in order to make progress, even in the face of sadness, it is also necessary to have something to look forward to. It can be something simple such as a concert, date or that book you've been dying to buy at the store. Regardless, it is necessary to have *something* to look forward to. It's also necessary to *hope*. So, with my small arsenal of snacks and barely working cassette deck to keep me company, the trip didn't seem quite as long and boring.

I remember arriving at her apartment building late that Friday night for the first time. Here I was. I was about to meet my friend in person. I think that I sat in my truck only long enough to make certain that I was parked legally and that my tires weren't buried too deep in the snow. I got out of my truck feeling simultaneously nervous and excited and walked to her apartment on the lower level of the building.

Our fondness for one another developed quickly in person. I noticed the radiance of her personality right away. I vividly recall her greeting me with an enormous hug as soon as I walked in the door.

We spent the majority of the weekend watching movies, television and listening to music as I recall. We "clicked" almost immediately so I knew that there must be something more substantial than a normal friendship there. However, I never would have imagined that on a subsequent visit, an event would occur that would change the both of our lives forever. Nevertheless, the weekend was coming to a close and I returned home that Sunday evening.

Two weeks had passed when I drove to Kansas again to visit Anne. There was no snow or ice on the highways so the bitter cold wasn't going to stop me. It was the fourth of December. After the first visit, we joked on the phone and on the internet chat about being sexually active. I knew for certain from the moment that I opened the door to her apartment that something was going to happen.

It was around three in the morning when I arrived. She stood there with glitter on her face and with her right eyebrow turned upward in an adorable manner. Her lustrous eyes put the winter moonlight to shame. I was once again greeted with a huge hug.

The floor of her bedroom was cluttered with books, magazines, clothes and a wide array of other items. She had a huge walk-in closet that was painted white and covered with glow-in-the-dark stars which were spread out in no particular order. This was where she slept, where we slept together and where a new life would be created.

She was playing the "Darkest Days" CD by the band Stabbing Westward on the CD-Rom drive of her computer. It played continuously throughout the morning. How ironic and prophetic was that album title considering the days that were to follow the abortion?

For the most part we were careful during intercourse. I did use protection. There were, however, a few seconds in the heat of passion when I did not. We believed that it was in those few seconds that we conceived a life.

At some point during that day we casually discussed what she would do in the event she became pregnant. I vividly remember sitting beside her on her bedroom carpet having this conversation with her and having to move books and magazines from the clutter of items so that I could sit. I do have to stop and wonder if our intuitions were telling us that we had just conceived a life. However, it could have been that we just realized that there were a few seconds when we had no protection and that we should probably discuss what would happen in the event that she did become pregnant.

She told me that if she became pregnant, she would choose to abort the child. There were several reasons why she would make this decision, she said. The most significant reason she gave, however, was that she felt she wasn't *ready* to be a mother and that I wasn't *ready* to be a father. She was only 20 and had just begun her 2nd year of college. I still had my pizza delivery job 300 miles away. It had only been a couple of weeks since we met in person, so we were no where close to discussing the idea of moving in together or the possibility of marriage. That discussion wouldn't take place for about two more months.

It has always felt more natural to me for whatever reason to look after the well-being of others before looking after myself. At times this has, quite honestly, come at a price to my own well-being. While I knew that it was her body and ultimately her decision, she hadn't inquired about how I felt about the situation. To be completely honest, I wasn't exactly communicating my opinions or concerns either. I kept quiet because I was putting her thoughts and feelings before anything else, even my own thoughts and feelings. Moreover, as a man, I knew that I had virtually no legal right or recourse to protect that child's life.

One of the main feelings which would tear away at my soul for the next few years was the fact that I neglected to defend the life of the baby. I also regret that I wasn't more vocal about my own feelings regarding the baby and the abortion. I was incapable or rather, unwilling to forgive myself for this for the longest period of time, several years in fact. I knew from early on that ultimately it would be her decision to choose either to keep the baby or to proceed with the abortion. However, I am certain that my process of healing might have been considerably easier if I had asserted my true feelings and wishes – if I had put up more of a fight.

I wish I could say I did defend the baby's life but I can't. Even if it wouldn't have made a difference, I could have looked back and said that I had at least made an effort. I believe that I was just overwhelmed with the fact that I was in the middle of a situation and I didn't know really *how* I should react. Creating a life was something that I had only imagined prior to my relationship with Anne and I never imagined that I would be discussing aborting that same life. I felt like the proverbial "deer caught in the headlights." However, it was for that very same reason that I would eventually realize that I *had* to forgive myself. I had to stare at myself in the rear-view mirror and realize that I wasn't the only man to whom this had happened. I also had to force myself to realize that I wasn't the only person who had dealt with feelings of guilt, regret, anger, sadness and anxiety when coping with the loss of a child to abortion.

While the *unknown* on the road ahead can be somewhat scary and intimidating, what's far worse and usually longer-lasting is living with a back that's breaking by the burden of regrets.

So, regret was one of the first emotions that I felt. Regret started shortly after the initial conversation in her bedroom. The anger wouldn't come to the surface until several weeks after the abortion. That's when the reality of what had happened had a chance to sink in and make a temporary home inside the cracks of my breaking soul.

** ** **

"I'm distant ... I fade, so far now ... away
my eyes fade, sink hard, so frozen, so far

I don't think that I will ever feel the same
and I don't think that this day will ever fade
I'm so frozen and so caught up in this day
I'm so frozen and so lost in this cold day"

Lycia – "Frozen"

** ** **

THE DAY OF THE PHONE CALL

I have traveled when the temperatures outside were well below freezing. I have been caught driving in storms of ice and freezing rain. However, the day of the phone call brought forth the coldest moment in my life.

Sometime during the two to three weeks prior to that cold day, she had taken two or three different pregnancy tests. One

19

or two tests produced positive results and a couple produced negative results. Additionally, she had already made an appointment with her primary care doctor for a routine check up, so she would get a definitive answer at that time.

THE CALL

I can recall that cold December day when she called me to tell me "the news." In fact, I can still recall it as though it just happened yesterday. The wind was whistling outside of the house and icicles above the front porch looked like swords of glass, occasionally falling and shattering into hundreds of pieces. On the floor to the left of my bed laid my telephone and answering machine. I awoke sometime between the hours of 9 and 10 AM. There was a message left on my voice mail. Barely awake, I reached down over the side of my bed and nervously pressed the "Play" button.

I had a number of Anne's voice mail messages recorded onto a cassette tape so that I could hear her voice when I was living 300 miles away from her. At that time, the sound of her voice on the tape provided for me a sense of comfort as it reminded me that I would see her again soon. The only chilling message on that cassette is the one that she left upon returning from her doctor's appointment that cold Saturday morning. Here's a transcript of that message:

"(sigh) … Hi, um, Will. It's me. I really really really need to talk to you. So whenever you get home, please give me a call … (sigh)..and um, I'm going to be gone for a little bit today cuz I have to go to the other doctor, so I'll talk to you later? Bye...." (hangs up phone)

When I heard that message, I had a pretty good idea of what she was going to tell me when I would call her back. My heart started beating as fast as the whistling wind outside and my stomach felt like it sank to a level equal to the depth of a ditch off of the side of the highway. Nevertheless, I returned her call though I was not yet fully awake. She was sobbing on the phone. Her doctor had performed an ultrasound examination and discovered a life approximately three weeks into development growing inside of her. I had fathered a child. Needless to say, all words failed me at that point.

I remember the light streaming in the window between the curtains in my bedroom that morning. My down comforter should have been a shield for the cold. However, it provided no protection for the onset of numbness that I started to feel in my soul.

I *should have* been happy to be a father anticipating the birth of my child. I was *supposed* to be overwhelmed with joy. Instead I became overwhelmed with severe anticipatory grief.

As soon as I heard the click that signaled the end of the call, my mind was thrown into a whirlwind of emotions. Perhaps either a "flash flood" or a "tornado warning" would be a more appropriate description. As I said before, the first and really only thing that I could think to do was to support her regardless of her decision, though I felt I had a good idea of what her decision was going to be.

As I previously mentioned, I had only imagined what it would be like to be expecting a child. I never expected that I would be discussing this child's abortion. So, most of my hopes and expectations were turned upside down that cold morning. The state of mind I was experiencing was most likely the reason I wasn't sure how to react. This was not supposed to be me in this position, I thought.

It should have been a moment to feel joy, but I felt a cold, sharp stab in my soul as I felt I knew the fate of our baby. It felt as though someone had taken an icicle like the ones hanging over my front porch and stabbed me directly in my soul.

Though I was a college graduate still with the unfortunate job of delivering pizzas, I was preparing myself to support our child if she did decide to not terminate the pregnancy. That is, even though I knew it would nearly kill me emotionally to be so far away from our baby. That was another assumption I made; that the baby would remain with her. Maybe I assumed this because the child usually ends up with the mother when single parents live apart. Though I thought the chance would be slim, I did regret not asking her to carry the baby to term and allowing me to raise it.

I also found myself in a position where I was fully prepared to give my life in exchange for this child's life. After all, I had lived nearly 25 years and this child hadn't even been provided with a chance to live yet. Who was I to waste perhaps a bit too much of my time on earth and this child didn't have a chance yet? If God would have walked out of the gates of Heaven over to me and told me that there was a near-perfect chance that my child would be born healthy and be provided with a good life, I would have made my Will and Testament and left this world without a moment for question or hesitation.

Maybe I wasn't selfish because I was supporting her regardless of her decision. Maybe it wasn't selfish of me to want to trade places with the baby. I don't know. I was keeping most of my thoughts and emotions on the matter from her. I had resigned to accepting the baby's fate though I was never comfortable with it by any stretch of the imagination. This took me years to come to terms with.

** ** **

THE COLD DAYS AFTER THE CALL

The seasons came and went as usual in the months and years thereafter. I should have been filled with joy and anticipation that I was going to become a father. Instead, what I was filled with was a sadness the likes of which I had never known until this point in my life.

There were a handful of moments that I can recall as if they occurred yesterday though the sequence of the events is a little blurry. There was no conceivable way that I could have kept a healthy journal during the days immediately following the abortion. I was too close to the situation. I needed to arrive at a safe distance away from the tragedy to get more of a healthy perspective. I needed time for the reality of the abortion to set in so that I could really feel the gravity of the situation, how I felt about it and how I was going to heal from the loss. That is, if I was going to be able to heal.

The term "snapshot" was originally a hunting term. To someone writing a memoir, this seems to be a very appropriate term. Think of how many hours hunters spend in the woods. Then consider the number of hours a writer spends "hunting" for the perfect words, digging up old memories, documenting them and forming a cohesive body of work.

I chose to organize part of this story with scenes or "snapshots" of my experiences. Some of these are from Kansas while others are from home.

** ** **

SNAPSHOTS AT HOME

Some of the snapshots at home that I recall revolve around phone conversations that I had with Anne. I can recall having a number of phone conversations with her in the days immediately following that day when she told me she was pregnant. In particular, two examples stick out in my mind.

In one case, I found myself in bed covered completely by my flannel sheets and with my phone to my ear. I was speaking softly to Anne but crying my eyes out. My body felt warm under the covers but my soul felt as frigid as the below-zero weather outside the house. I recall the unwelcome morning light streaming in from the sides of the curtains on my two windows.

Nothing existed under those covers except that baby and its mother's voice on the other end of the phone. As far as I was concerned I didn't exist anymore. My world was destroyed.

Perhaps the most painful of my memories during the days before the abortion were those conversations when she would tell me what "she and the baby" were going to do that week. It was very strange to hear. Here was a woman who was planning to have an abortion, yet she was talking in such a nurturing manner like a mother who was going about her daily business of taking care of a baby.

On one occasion, I can recall sitting on a small wooden chair in my basement with my bare feet touching the cold cement floor. During our conversation, Anne said things like, "Well, we're going to go eat and then jump in the hot tub for a while." This was just one example of these kinds of conversations. It was the "we" part that drove the icicle through my heart.

The thing I remember most of those conversations with her was the fact that I was often crying my eyes out although being somewhat quiet about it so she wouldn't hear how damaged I felt. It felt almost like a muffled scream, like someone had gagged me and tied a cloth around my head. Inside I was crying loud. However, when I was in the company of most of my friends, family or co-workers, I was holding back or putting on a facade.

During another conversation, she said "We're going to lie down in front of the stereo speakers and listen to daddy's tape." I had given her a cassette on which I had three songs recorded. Sometimes I like to think that the reason that I often hear melodies in my head is because my angel is sending me parts of heavenly melodies from somewhere, perhaps as a return favor for whatever reason.

I also had to question, though Anne seemed so nurturing, if she was completely confident that proceeding with the abortion was the right thing to do. I'm sure she probably meant no ill-will during those conversations but they were very strange and painful nonetheless.

A good man will always consider and respect his wife's or his girlfriend's feelings before his, but he should always speak his own feelings as well. Otherwise, if he's encountering emotions such as those that may occur after experiencing the abortion of his child, he will find himself in a self-imposed emotional hell like the one I found myself in. It would be a long and often ice-covered road before arriving at a place of peace after feeling the regrets of not speaking my mind and not voicing objection to the abortion. I'm not saying it would have made any difference. It might not have and it might not make a difference in someone else's life. However, the most piercing of regrets is the knowing that I didn't make much of an effort.

The next step was telling my parents. Added to the weight of all that I was experiencing was the burden of informing them that their grandchild would not be born. I don't really recall the exact words my dad chose when I spoke to him. However, I am certain that I told him. I am also certain that he was very supportive and offered to listen if or when I needed to vent. I could always count on him for that.

I don't know what felt worse: either keeping the news from my mother or, actually telling her why I had been so upset during recent days. I couldn't keep it inside any longer. I asked her to come into my room and I then told her, "Anne's having an abortion and it's mine." She must have sat there at my bedside crying along side of me and listening to me for the better part of an hour. I recall her offering of help in the event Anne decided to keep the baby. Like most of my best friends, she accepted that I was going to go through what I had to and in my own way. When I walked out the front door at night to walk along the snow-packed paths in the nearby woods, she asked only one question; "Did you remember your hat and gloves?" As it has always been the case, she was there for me without condition when I needed her or when I simply needed someone to listen.

I knew that my mother always wanted grandchildren. Breaking the news to her that I was partially responsible for creating a life that would shortly be taken away from us was extraordinarily painful. So was the expression on her face as she quietly walked out of my bedroom.

** ** **

"The window is open. You have to face the fear
Reaching out for solitude. It's no way near
From now on your life will never be the same

Black as the touch of a painful depression
You struggle to get to your destination
Strokes of a white brush will be your salvation

Avoiding reflections of traumatizing scars
Your grasping at straws and reaching for the stars
Your heart has been ruptured and it will never heal"

Leaether Strip – "Black Candle"

** ** **

THE DAY OF THE ABORTION

I once heard someone say, "You will never know silence and loneliness until you find yourself in a spacecraft as the power fails." Think of the shock of the power failure and the feeling that no one could reach you nor could you reach anyone. Imagine the degree of loneliness and the idea that you might never come back from the state of mind you're in. Imagine the idea of dying alone, not just physically but perhaps more importantly, emotionally.

That was how I felt on Saturday, January 2, 1999. In spite of the fact that I felt Anne had already made her decision, nothing could prepare me for the moment I received that phone call after she returned home from just having the abortion. I was barely awake when she called. However, I was coherent enough to feel the deepest emotional emptiness that I had ever experienced. It was done, confirmed. Our child, our angel was dead. The guilt and regret that I had been feeling since the phone call after she found out she was pregnant now grew three-fold. A massive gaping wound had opened up inside of me, one that I could never imagine being completely filled. I was supposed to be a dad. However, it felt like I was *dead.*

Though I hadn't been that fond of celebrating my birthday for several years, I felt that this year I had less reason to. How was I supposed to celebrate my 25th birthday when the day before was the day of my child's death? I felt absolutely no reason to celebrate.

I'm sure our angel couldn't feel pain during the abortion since it was only one month into its development. Nevertheless, that doesn't make the loss of our child any less real for me. It sure as Hell didn't matter when I had to combat the feelings of regret, failure, sadness, anger and guilt.

A part of me died on January 2, 1999. Period.

I felt terrible that I couldn't take the trip out to be with her the day she found out she was pregnant and the day she had the abortion. The roads between Illinois and Kansas were covered with ice and snow. I couldn't hold her hand, be by her side to comfort her or try to get her to change her decision at the last minute in case she was having second thoughts.

I also couldn't arrange a little memorial with her for our baby when she got home. I couldn't say goodbye to our angel. I had to write this book in order to do that.

Perhaps I was being smart regarding my own safety by not traveling on the icy roads to Kansas. However, a part of me has always felt a little selfish for not making an attempt.

In addition to the amount of time I was spending dealing with my own thoughts and emotions, I also spent a countless number of hours thinking about what she was going through. I wanted to know what she was thinking and feeling. I believe the reason I devoted so much time to these thoughts was that by doing so, I felt that a part of me could magically take away some of the hurt or discomfort the abortion likely brought into her life. If I could "understand" as best I could from miles away, I felt may help ease some of her pain. In retrospect I think it was just part of my grieving process. I've always faced grief head-on even if by doing so, my thoughts crossed the line of obsession.

She told me briefly about the office where she had the abortion. I could imagine the office-a slightly less than stellar environment probably in a not-so-great part of the city and the crabby receptionist who's perhaps looking more forward to the end of her day than assisting the patients in the clinic. According to an article in the journal *Family Relations*, one father whose child died from abortion described his grief this way:

"I wasn't in the room; I wasn't even in the clinic that day. But in my mind I've been there a million times since. I've been there watching, breaking, wanting to rescue you. In my mind I need to be a hero not a killer, the man who didn't flee. But I am not. I am the man I fear I see."

I thought about those men in the waiting room of the clinic and what was likely going through their minds. I also thought about those men who tried to force their wives or girlfriends into getting an abortion. I thought about the fact that some men probably vehemently opposed the procedures but were there for their partners anyway. I wanted to know what these men were thinking, what their fears were, their regrets and if they were perhaps battling demons similar to the ones I was battling.

Additionally, I thought of the men who weren't there in the waiting room. Those were likely the ones who either deserted their partners after learning of the pregnancy or felt like they couldn't handle the experience of being at the clinic. Sure, those are speculations, but reasonable ones I believe.

I thought about all of those men whether they were in the office where the abortion of their child was taking place or not. There was however, one central thought that crossed my mind about all of those men. That was the fact that most of them probably felt like they didn't have a voice, a way to understand what they were going through nor did they know what to say or do for their wives or girlfriends.

I spent a lot of hours trying to imagine what it must have been like for Anne during the procedure. I also wondered if she was having second thoughts even at the last second before the abortion. A small part of me wondered if she was maybe waiting for me to stand up and voice my opposition to the abortion.

I think some part of me wanted to not only understand her feelings but to also punish myself for my responsibility in creating a life that she chose to take away from us. If I was ever going to come out of this situation a mentally healthy individual, I had to understand what she went through and what I was going through. This is where time comes in. Because you can't always see things clearly until time has passed and you look in that rear view mirror.

I've wondered what happened to the remains of the baby after the abortion took place; if they were disposed of respectfully or if they were tossed carelessly among the thousands of other lost hopes and dreams. Regardless, our baby was released into the same winter wind that brought it to us.

** ** **

THE DAYS AFTER THE ABORTION

The Drawing

Why she made a drawing of the sonogram I'll never know. I'll never know a lot of what she thought and felt but I guess that's okay now. Nevertheless, she drew the picture of the baby, scanned it and emailed me a copy. I was very grateful for that.

I sincerely wanted to be with her at the doctor's office when she initially found out that she was pregnant. More importantly, though, I wanted to be there when she had the abortion. Since I wasn't though, at the very minimum, I wanted to know what she was going through and I wanted to accept as much of her trauma as possible. I was always raised to be an unselfish person. However, sometimes you can cross a line between unselfish and completely avoiding one's own health and well being. That's what happened with me. Nevertheless, the drawing of the sonogram was the closest thing to an actual photo that I have had. I'll be forever grateful to her for giving that to me.

She supposedly wrote a letter to our child in the days following the abortion. I only wished I had a copy of that letter. Though I asked her for a copy, I never received one. Again, I wanted to understand things from her perspective. I wanted to know if her thoughts and feelings regarding the abortion were similar to mine. I wondered if she experienced regret, depression or the seemingly endless what-could-have-beens like I experienced.

While the occasions were rare, from time to time a flash of thought made me think that it would be foolish to be distraught, dwell on or to devote time to writing this book since the baby was only four weeks into its development when the abortion occurred. However, all I need to do is return to the drawing of the sonogram that she gave to me. It plants the hole back in my heart and reminds me of the reality of the situation. It reminds me that life, in and of itself is sacred.

In a manner of speaking, it represents my long time hopes being destroyed. Yet, it also represents hope for the future. Those were partly my eyes, my hands and my heart that had just barely begun to form. It's been a long–time argument as to what point an actual live being is formed. However, when one can see on a screen a body beginning to form, I don't understand how you could argue.

In some ways, I think that this book might not have been written had it not been for Anne giving me a copy of that drawing. That drawing helped the reality set in. It allowed me to face my grief, anger and every other nasty emotion that was cluttering my heart. For a while, I hung a copy of that drawing above the door to my room. This was a reminder to walk out of the clutter of the bedroom and get a different perspective on the mess that my heart had become.

** ** **

GOING BACK TO KANSAS

The trips to Kansas were different now. By this time Anne had moved into her parents' house. The trips were starting to seem longer. The anticipation that once made the trips go by relatively quickly was now slowly diminishing with each trip. The sounds of the Mamas and the Papas and Jim Croce that came from the cassette deck were of less company and were more of a distraction now.

Before I went back to Kansas to visit Anne, I wrote a letter to her parents. I believe it was between three and four pages in length. It was important to me to make it clear to her parents that I was going to do my best to be supportive of their daughter. I also didn't want to lose their respect. I remember explaining to them that if given the opportunity, I would have traded places with that child. I would have traded my life for that of the child and all of the pain and stress that Anne was under. I don't know if my letter made any difference in regard to their feelings about me. They never mentioned it when I saw them on subsequent visits. Quite honestly, it was a rather strange feeling going to their house after the abortion had occurred. The abortion was never discussed between her parents and me nor was it discussed much between Anne and me either. After the first or second trip back to Kansas after the abortion, I really started to feel like I didn't belong there anymore.

The bi-weekly trips to see Anne after the abortion would only happen for the next four months. Initially, her mother didn't want me to come to visit until I had paid the full cost of the abortion. While I paid part of the cost, eventually Anne convinced her mother to allow me to come out to visit anyway. That's another thing that ate at my heart for a while-the fact that I *paid* for part of the cost of the abortion. Yet, at that time I wanted to be there for her and I was initially under the assumption that I wouldn't be allowed to visit unless I paid the full cost.

I was also no longer going to see my girlfriend. I was driving to be with the woman whom I made a mother, a woman who took away our child.

I can recall the first time I saw her after the abortion. It would have been the first week of February, 1999. Again, she stood there with her right eyebrow pointed upward in its unique way. However, her once lucid eyes now seemed as though they had become filled with clouds of confusion and bereavement. The initial hug seemed like it lasted a lifetime. I know we both had a pretty good cry then. I would have been inclined to believe that the loss of our child might have brought us closer together. However, I think the abortion was ultimately a factor in the end of my relationship with Anne. In fact, I'm certain of it.

** ** **

SNAPSHOTS IN KANSAS

As I mentioned, visits to Kansas would never be the same again. To me, everywhere Anne and I went became a place that we couldn't take our baby. If we went to a restaurant, it wasn't just a place to go eat lunch or dinner. It was a place where we couldn't take the baby or perhaps feed it in a high chair. If we went for a walk through the woods, the walk became one in which we didn't take the baby in a stroller down the wooded path. We couldn't do anything or go anywhere without my brain thinking that it was something we did *without* the baby.

It would be like this for a while, at least from my perspective. It would be a long while before I would begin to view areas of my life being of "me" and not just "without the baby." For a long while, I would view my world as a collection of "what-could-have- beens;" a clutter like her old bedroom floor.

The Glass Angel

On one occasion when I went to Kansas to see Anne, she gave me an angel that she made from small shards of a mirror that were then glued to a piece of foam. This must have been around February or March of 1999. The angel was barely glued to the foam. How ironic-(or perhaps somewhat symbolic) was its composition dependant on the foam backing, yet so unsecured. While I have often been accused of being over-analytical, I couldn't help but find the mirror to be somewhat symbolic.

The edges of the broken mirror were sharp. It was like looking at my emotions at the time; a broken reflection of me with sharp edges like a knife to the soul. Still the pieces were quite rudimentary, like the basic elements of our lives with which we should really be concerned. A few years after she gave me this glass angel, I opened a shoebox I had placed it in for storage. A piece had nearly come off the foam so it had to be re-glued.

** ** **

One of the most memorable "snapshots" from Kansas that I can recall was the same visit during which she gave me the glass angel. We were alone in her room in her parents' house. The floor was cluttered as it was in her room in her old apartment; clothes and other miscellaneous items strewn about. One of these items was a furry white stuffed gorilla toy with a red heart that I had given to her for Valentine's Day.

I brought with me a cassette tape which included the instrumental versions of three new songs I had been working on. I wanted to play the tape for her and see what sort of reaction or feeling she got from just the instrumental versions. I think I intended this to be somewhat of a test. I wanted to see how she would connect with the art into which I pour my soul. Maybe I indirectly meant it as a test to see whether or not she and I were meant to be.

I didn't tell her the names of the songs. I just let them play. I was most curious about what her impression would be of one song in particular. That song was "Forward to My Unborn," the last song on the cassette. We lay there silently and listened.

After listening to the three songs, she said that she was left with a feeling that was rather atmospheric. She said she could envision herself in the woods or somewhere with the wind blowing or snow falling around. I was delighted that she had this reaction. After all, the mood I've always attempted to create in my music has definitely been one that can either be described as "atmospheric" or even "ethereal." Moreover, the woods in the middle of winter have always been one of my favorite places to be.

Nevertheless, while we were listening to "Forward to My Unborn" she told me how parts of the song sounded sad, or as though someone could possibly be crying during those parts. The feeling she described brought to mind a private place where one would go away from the world to be alone, to cry, to pray or to just let themselves fall apart for a while. That's exactly what I did from time to time after the abortion.

There were times during the first couple of winters in the years following the abortion where I would escape from my everyday world and seek the solace of the woods near my mother's house. I could spend an hour or two, sometimes even longer in those woods. I would move the frost-covered branches out of my way and breathe the winter air as I walked through the meandering snow-covered paths. There was something very peaceful and quite honestly, rather spiritual about those walks.

ONE LAST SNAPSHOT FROM
KANSAS: THE LAST VISIT

In retrospect, I think that deep down inside I knew it would be my last visit to Kansas. I think that I knew I was going there to break up with Anne. However, I ignored the voice inside my head and went anyway. Though I don't recall behaving in a strange manner, she said that I had acted strangely that weekend. I do, however, recall *feeling* very much at odds though. This was four months after the abortion and the gravity of it was really starting to affect me significantly. I recall feeling pulled mentally and emotionally in different directions. I knew that I still loved her, or at least I thought that I did. However, the resentment and anger toward her following the abortion had increased. I began to lose the knowledge of who I was as a person. I was also nowhere close to getting any answers about how I should handle the experience of the abortion. So, needless to say, my conviction regarding my future with Anne was becoming less and less solid as the days went on.

To be completely honest, there was really only one brief moment of clarity during that entire weekend.

I vividly recall standing out in her back yard one night staring at the open Kansas sky. Winter's chill had faded and spring's breeze had arrived. I thought of the days when I would travel to visit her at her old apartment. I thought of how the appearance of her apartment was cluttered yet things *felt* right and in order to me. However, as I looked up at the Kansas sky, with its clarity and organization of stars in constellations, nothing *felt* right inside of me.

I felt that while our angel was created among the clutter of the walk-in closet below the scattered stars, it had been released into the universe among the order of the constellations. For a moment, I felt that our angel was okay.

In other words, the duality of appearance versus inner feelings became very apparent to me at that moment. Where I once found myself among clutter, though feeling ok on the inside, I now found myself with a small sense of the order of the world around me, yet inside I felt scattered and lost. Simply put, I felt like a stranger in a strange land.

During one of our last conversations in person, we arrived on the subject of getting married. Originally, a friend of mine from Chicago was going to marry us. The fact is that it had been bothering me for some time that she was an atheist and didn't seem open to other beliefs. Though I would never personally hold someone's spiritual beliefs against them, I couldn't enter into a union which I believe *should* be spiritual with someone who didn't believe in God. It's like a person could recite the words but they wouldn't really believe them. So, when she asked me if my friend would come down at that moment and marry us if I would go through with it, I couldn't give her a definite "Yes." Needless to say, that would be the last conversation I would have with Anne in person.

I distinctly recall the last drive home from Kansas and how long it seemed to last. It had nothing to do with the traffic or weather either. My relationship with Anne was over. I came to the realization that I had to go forth on this journey a lone traveler. I remember "looking in the rear-view mirror" and reflecting on my relationship with Anne. I didn't regret the time I spent with her. However, I did feel some sense of regret with regard to not taking the time to really know her before we rushed into our relationship.

On my way home, I stopped at a Borders store to see if they had the latest Human Drama album, "Solemn Sun Setting." They didn't. Shame on them, by the way. Though I didn't really think about it at the time, that title was a very descriptive of how I felt. I prayed for the sun to set so sleep could welcome me. Even then, the realms of sleep and dreams weren't always a safe place for me. Many of my dreams were filled with images of the child I never had and symbols of the loss I felt.

Nevertheless, when morning came I cursed the sunrise and the light that came into my window.

About 18 months later I began writing..........

** ** **

"My beloved do you know, how many times I stared at clouds thinking that I saw you there."

VNV Nation - "Beloved"

** ** **

MORE SNAPSHOTS AT HOME

These snapshots are perhaps few, but are nonetheless very vivid.

One winter night in January of 1999, I recall walking on the sidewalk outside of my house. The snow was shiny from the light of the street lights and the tightly-packed snow crunched underneath my feet on the sidewalk. As I walked past my truck, I could see my shadow to my left near the street. It appeared almost like a smaller figure; a child walking behind me. As I moved, so did the shadow.

Similarly, my mode of thinking at that time was that I didn't want to let go, or rather that I *couldn't* let go of everything that I thought and felt after the abortion. It was as though I could see a shadow behind me at all times, regardless of whether it was during the day or night. I think it was around this time that I started to wonder if all that I could do was to nurture the memory or rather, the "what-could-have-beens." Nevertheless, that "shadow" will always be behind me for the rest of my life. It would also teach me to walk in new ways.

I vividly recall another "snapshot" from another winter night. I was standing a few inches deep in the snow at the edge of our yard clearing the snow and ice off of my truck. It was late at night and the only other signs of life were the sounds of an occasional car on the main stretch of road through town one block away. I became overwhelmed with sadness due to the loss of the baby, the lost opportunities and the ever- present "what-could-have-beens." I can recall scraping the ice off of my windshield as the lyrics to a very poignant song called "Winter's Life" by the band Human Drama ran through my head:

"...the mist that wets my face will surely freeze by sundown..
As sure as winter comes, it drags with it, its sadness.

...but all has changed. I feel a new heart beat. In your eyes I'll always see Winter's Life.

You are the warmth I feel through the coldest December, the single ray of sun that shines on a cloudy day. You are the proof that heaven answers...the fire to warm my freezing hands...and the color on the greyest of days.

Love rain down on me. Erase the weight of the world. Climb upon my shoulder.
You are the weight of my world.
I'll suffer the wind and with each shiver remember...winter is not the end, but a reminder.....that a brilliant day is on the horizon.....and as each year goes by, so builds my treasure of love.

All has changed. I feel a new heartbeat.
In your eyes, I'll always see Winter's Life."

I'd like to mention what these words have meant to me and the symbolism that I found within them.

I've always been fond of the winter season, at least some aspects of it. The leafless trees glazed with snowflakes as well as the quiet snow-covered landscapes untouched by footprints often create the most beautiful atmospheres. I've never quite understood why so many people seem to experience seasonal depression during the winter season. I've always found it to be an inspirational and beautiful time of the year. At the very least it's a season of diversity; the delicate snowflakes on the bare trees in contrast to the abrasive ice storms and loud snowplows driving down the streets. I've often joked with my mother about the reason I enjoy winter perhaps more than most people I meet; the fact that I was born in January in the middle of an ice storm. The name that I used in the chat room where I met Anne was, in fact "Winter." I also used "winter" in my band name, *In Winter*

Bleeding though a common misconception is that I thought of that name after the winter of 1998/1999 and after the abortion. I didn't. I thought of it several months before then.

As I understand, Johnny Indovina of Human Drama wrote the song "Winter's Life" for a friend whose wife had given birth to a baby during the winter season. However, one of the many beauties of art is that often, limitless interpretations of a lyric or piece of music may be gathered by each listener.

For me, the song "Winter's Life" meant so many different things during this time.

It represented for me the sadness of the passing of our child's life and the ending of the season through which our baby arrived and left. It also provided for me a feeling of looking forward to the season to follow and the celebration of life in a brand new light. That was something I desperately needed at the time, even if the light during this time was at the end of a very long tunnel that I was to walk through.

** ** **

THE STORM BEFORE THE CALM

I liken the first few months, even the first couple of years after the abortion to driving in the middle of a winter storm in a new truck that's just being broken in. It's as if I were driving through patches of fog, with rear wheel drive instead of four wheel drive while the tires and alignment are becoming faulty from all of the pot holes. While having the ice freezing on my windshield, the wipers are fighting to help me clearly see the road in front of me. After all, the visibility isn't more than a car length or two. That's the best way to describe it. I was basically on auto-pilot.

There was no rule book or manual telling me what to do or how to deal with all that I was thinking and feeling. That's probably why so many men keep their post-abortion stress hidden, because there's no single "How-To" manual. If such a manual did exist though, it would likely have diagrams and numbers listed next to the parts indicating the quantity of sadness, anger, resentment or despair which should be included. Unfortunately, life's not so easy and the pathway to healing from abortion for men and women is more like an open field of grief where you have to do your best to navigate where you are going through the snow.

When I began writing this book, there were only a handful of resources for men dealing with post-abortion trauma, some of which I didn't even realize existed until some time had passed during my writing. With each article and book that is written on the subject of post-abortion trauma, the "pathway" in that "open field" of grief becomes that much easier to navigate through. In my case, the more articles, books and testimonials by or for men who've endured post-abortion trauma that I read, the easier it was for me to see where I was "driving." Most importantly though, the more I read, the less "alone" I felt. At some point, I realized that the thoughts and emotions I was experiencing after the abortion where not so unique to my situation. In fact, more often than not, many men it seemed experienced very similar thoughts and emotions.

There were a number of emotions that I had to struggle with for a while. I had already been feeling the pierce of guilt and the weight of regret. A few months after guilt and regret, anger began to surface as did a number of other emotions.

ANGER

I was angry with Anne for taking the life of our child, yet I was also angry with myself for not fighting for the child's life. I tried my best to be supportive of her at the time as that was what came naturally to me. However, I had a growing feeling of resentment toward her not only for not giving the child a chance, but also for telling me things such as "what she and the baby did" or "what they were going to do. It was like driving an icicle right through my heart. Also, I never received the one thing that I asked for from her, which was a letter she had supposedly written to the baby. As I tried to understand what she was going through, I never was really given that chance. I only had a glimpse once in a while on the internet chat.

ENVY

For at least a year or more, every time I saw a parent, especially a father with their little son or daughter, I became very envious. When I had my pizza delivery job years ago, every time I would go to the door and a child would answer, I would imagine that house being mine and my child answering the door. Those families had everything I ever wanted in my life-a home, a child; a family of my own.

FEAR

Until well after I had begun the process of healing by journaling, I was afraid. I was scared to get involved in another relationship because I knew that if I had to endure another abortion, I would likely have to be committed to a mental health facility. I was afraid of getting too close to someone only to be let down. I was also scared of falling into the pattern of not disclosing my true inner feelings and thoughts, regardless of the nature of the issue.

ANXIETY

Anxiety actually started around the time of the initial conversation Anne and I had in her bedroom. I was anxious and consumed with anticipatory grief until the day of the abortion. Afterward, I recall much of the time being on edge and unable to relax whenever I had a problem or concern. I don't know the exact point at which this one ceased. However, anxiety was definitely one of the more obnoxious demons to deal with.

GUILT & REGRET

I'm putting the two of these together. I deal with guilt and regret in greater detail later in this book. Guilt and regret were the first demons to arrive and the last to leave. They were, without question, the most cumbersome and heart-wrenching.

I don't think I was really aware of much of what I was thinking and feeling until a little while after the abortion. It took some time to be able to put labels on my emotions.

I was driving but I had no idea what the destination was going to be. There was no one that I knew of who had been through this so I didn't know where to turn or who to turn to. It was Hell to say the least. I wish I could say that I was able to flip a switch one day and suddenly realize why I had to deal with the abortion and what I needed to do to heal. I wish I could tell someone where to go to find the light switch. Unfortunately, grief and depression don't work like that. I had to *work* my way through.

** ** **

FAILURE AS A MAN AND FATHER

Feeling like a failure is not something that I have ever taken lightly. I don't like the feeling of letting myself down. More importantly, I don't enjoy the feeling of letting others down. Nevertheless, after the abortion I felt like the biggest failure as a man and as a father. I let myself down. I let my family down. Most importantly, I let that baby down as well as anyone that might have gotten to know him or her. So that's how I felt. I viewed myself as a direct and indirect failure.

What kind of a man was I? I often asked this of myself. What kind of man would not speak his true thoughts and emotions or stick up for his own wishes? What kind of man gives up without a fight? Men are supposed to be strong and I was not. I felt like

43

I just let the abortion happen. Unfortunately, in all too many cases, I believe men who've lost children to abortion feel very similar to this.

I also questioned my ability as a father. I felt like a failure as a father because I didn't stick up for the life of my child. I failed to protect the baby. I didn't even so much as make an attempt. For a long time after the abortion I wondered if maybe I didn't deserve to be or wasn't supposed to be a father. Parents are supposed to protect their children first and I felt that I didn't make an effort. As time slowly drug its feet I tried to not beat myself up for this. However, not beating myself up was difficult in and of itself.

Failure can either hurl someone into submission or drive them to succeed. In my case, my feelings of failure did both. Failure helped lower the rope to the depths of the pit I ended up in. However, with every month that passed and with every word that I wrote down for this book, failure helped show the cracks and ledges where I could put my feet and eventually reach the top again.

** ** **

THE WHAT IFs and WHAT COULD HAVE BEENs

Perhaps the most unsettling of feelings that I dealt with for the longest period of time were the feelings of all of the "what-might-have-beens" and "what-ifs." There were days and nights that were filled with any number of those. I was drowning in the proverbial glass half-empty, periodically sticking my head above the water in the glass half-full.

Another thing that's extremely difficult to deal with after suffering a loss (in any case, not just abortion) is the amount of unanswered questions and the thoughts that remain after a tie is severed.

At one point I made a partial list of some of my guilty feelings and regrets. I also made a partial list of unanswered questions. Often times, I would not just think about them, but I would think TOO much about them.

Partial list of guilt and regrets:
- Being partially responsible for a life that was lost
- Not being fully protected
- Not being there when she had the ultrasound
- Not being able to be there when she had the abortion
- Being partially responsible for causing a traumatic situation for a 20 year old girl
- For the pain it caused our parents
- For rushing into a relationship before I *really* knew Anne
- For not standing up for the child and voicing my opinions rather than blindly supporting her

List of Unanswered Questions:
- Would the child have been a boy or a girl?
- Would it have looked more like her or more like me?
- Would the child have been born healthy?
- Should I have encouraged her to get a second opinion regarding the child's health, and what would the doctor have said?
- What would the baby's first word have been?
- What would our lives have been like had the baby been born?
- Where would we have gone with our baby?
- What about all of the potential contributions to the world or community our baby might have offered?
- Where is the child's spirit: around us? in heaven?
- What would we have named our baby?

- Does our angel forgive us?

On any given day any number of these thoughts would flash repeatedly through my head. These thoughts became obsessions. The clouds were growing thicker and the sky was getting lower. That's why I had to write.

** ** **

"The Sun was born, so it shall die
So only shadows comfort me
I know in darkness I will find you giving up inside like me
Each day shall end as it begins
And though you're far away from me
I know in darkness I will find you giving up inside like me"

VNV Nation - "Further"

** ** **

THE LOWEST OF THE LOW

I think that I realized I needed to take all of my *thinking* and turn it into *action* when I hit emotional lows the likes of which I had never known before. This occurred about one year and a few months after the abortion and after my relationship with Anne had dissolved, right around the time when I started writing the Letters. While I have occasionally struggled with depression throughout my life, this was something that was very different from a simple chemical imbalance. This was something deeper. By this time, most of my feelings, or rather "demons" had a chance to manifest. All of the regret, anger, guilt, sadness and what-could-have-beens had plenty of time to nestle their way into my soul.

I have never contemplated suicide, at least *actively* ending it all. I have never firmly believed that I could go too far over the emotional edge and end my own life willfully. Even at my emotional lows after the abortion, I knew that I was blessed with a lot of things in my life, especially the unconditional love of my friends and family.

I do recall some considerably dark moments though. I remember nights when I would wonder what it would be like to fall asleep and not wake up. I also remember mornings when all I wanted to do was fall back asleep and not wake up again. My mode of thinking was this; maybe those who cared about me wouldn't resent me for dying by some means other than my own hand.

I wanted to be with my angel. That's all there was to it. I appreciated all of the blessings in my life, but what good were they if I had been partially responsible for the creation of a life; a miracle that was killed? Perhaps I deserved to suffer. Maybe I was supposed to go through this because I never at least **tried** to keep our child alive. I'd be willing to bet that many more men who've felt the regret of not trying to prevent their child's abortion have encountered similar feelings as well. That's probably what leads to irresponsible or erratic behavior in some men or even unsuccessful subsequent relationships.

For a while I couldn't eat right or sleep right. When I did sleep, many nights I would have bad dreams, some of which I discuss in the Letters section.

Occasionally I would hear a voice in my head that was telling me I was headed down a road leading to a heart attack before the age of thirty. Essentially, I was dying of a broken heart.

That's where my mentality was at the time. Rational thinking had been rained upon and washed down the dirty drain. These were, without question, the darkest days.

Documenting all of my thoughts and emotions during the months after the abortion was initially my way of survival. In fact, I'm not even sure I was consciously aware at first that I was doing it to survive emotionally. A bit later on I think I realized *why*. That was to survive, to live. I had no clue as to how to rise above and beyond my emotional hell. I didn't know *why* I had to survive. I certainly didn't feel that I deserved to. I just knew that I *had* to. I turned to the only tools of survival I could think of-a series of pens and notebooks.

Writing was like a rite of exorcism for me. However, the demons didn't come out right away. It was only through the progress of writing and editing, essentially controlling those demons that they were eventually expelled from my mind and onto the path of the marginally legible etchings in my notebook. In other words, I fought the beasts of depression, regret, anger, and sorrow with an ink-filled sword and blue-colored, college-ruled shield.

Somewhere along the line in composing this book after some of those demons had a chance to manifest, my obsession with the seemingly endless amount of "what if?" questions coupled with the mountain of guilt and regret, somehow developed into one basic question. That question was, "In what ways can I honor this child and celebrate life?"

** ** **

"Tonight we can live like there's no time left.
We just might find some meaning in the face of death.
The love you hold in your hands cries for life."

Ophelia's Sweet Demise -*"Crown in the Ground"*

** ** **

TURNING THE BAD INTO GOOD

Even post-traumatic stress and depression can have their limitations. Likewise, and strangely enough, happiness itself became uncomfortable because I spent hours, weeks, even months at a time in an emotional and psychological hell. While it's most certainly easier said than done at times, the key is to find some reasons, however small they may be, reasons to live and progress.

However, there needs to be two elements to this. The first is the active purging of all of the negative emotions and walking the steps toward mental sanity again. The second is the act of *doing* things. By this one I mean the act of performing a task or service for someone other than one's self.

Regarding the first element, the journal as a tool for survival became the one thing that I enjoyed doing when inspiration washed over me. Each word in the notebook was a "baby" step toward emotional survival and stability. I had to learn to walk again before reaching out to anyone else.

Regarding the second element, it also had to start with small things. I think that it has to for anyone who's lived in shoes like the ones I did at the time. It starts with things like reaching out of bed to the telephone and calling your significant other, or volunteering an hour or two per week for someone in need.

Slowly over time little events helped me to learn that I was going to have to live with the loss of the baby for the rest of my life. Accepting that and dealing with it was the next trick. There have definitely been both peaks as well as valleys.

I knew that I couldn't get our child back. I also knew that it was unrealistic to have traded places with the child. Somewhere along the line I decided that the best thing that I could do to honor this child was by not only writing this book, but also by doing a number of things for myself and for other people as well.

I would like to make something perfectly clear though. I don't provide these examples to put myself on a pedestal. I'm simply providing these as examples of things that could help get one through the healing process. I deal with that more in the Advise section in the Afterword.

TEDDY BEARS FOR THE KIDS

On a couple of occasions, I decided to donate some stuffed animals to local and state police departments. I may have looked a bit amusing walking through Target with my long hair and two armfuls of stuffed animals. However, I knew that police officers often gave them to children who were caught up in traumatic situations such as domestic violence. So, I gave back to other children and the community and therefore, honored the child I lost. I can recall leaving Target that day and being overcome with sad thoughts of my child. I also recall making a left-hand turn onto the main street on my way to the State Police office when it began to rain.

THE CHILDREN'S MUSEUM

Perhaps the time I most enjoyed was the time I spent working as a Museum Assistant for the Worldways Children's Museum in St. Louis. While it was a temporary position that lasted for only little over one month, it was indeed one of the most enjoyable and rewarding jobs I have ever had.

I recall the first time I walked in for my job interview. The museum looked incredible for the small space that it occupied. There were two different cultural exhibits where children could walk through and get a small glimpse of what it could be like as a person from either of those cultures. It's the kind of place that I would have loved as a child. I could envision myself bringing my own child there and smiling at the expressions of happiness and discovery in his or her eyes.

During my interview, I was told that my job would be to drive a rental truck around the county to a few schools where I would assist in assembling and dismantling the pieces of this mobile exhibit called the H2Orchestra. I had never driven a rental van before then and I wasn't fond of that idea so the interview was brief. A week or two later, the woman from the museum who interviewed me called to ask if I had, by any chance, given the job a second thought. She also told me that it would be just for the summer. I thought about it for a day and decided that the job must have been meant for me.

The H2Orchestra's components were different instruments that incorporated the use of water to produce musical and tonal sounds. For example, there was an instrument which used a metal gong that a child could dip in the water while hitting it and it would produce a variety of tones. Other examples included giant flutes that when dipped in tubs of water, would produce an array of musical notes. To most of the children, however, the exhibit served a secondary purpose. That was the splashing of large amounts of water on other children on those hot days.

We assembled the H2Orchestra at four different schools as I recall. The children would arrive class by class. The other assistants and I would then perform a demonstration for each class. After that, we would have the children rotate between instruments to improvise, or perhaps more importantly to them, splash water on themselves and other students. After approximately ten minutes, we'd give a couple of children the chance of conducting the orchestra. More descriptively, this was a flurry of improvisation and time for the children to drench themselves and those nearby. Perhaps painters like Jackson Pollock and musicians like Miles Davis would have been proud.

While I took this job only on a temporary basis, I will never forget it as long as I live. I can think of no better duty and service to humanity than playing even a small role in a child's discovery of any form of art. The expressions of discovery lit up in the eyes of many of those children made all of the hard work worth while. I recall kneeling down to assist little boys and girls with some of the instruments. This experience led me to feel that perhaps the most noble of pursuits is the service to children and the encouragement of their creativity.

I recall looking into the eyes of many of these small children and simultaneously feeling a great sense of gratitude for all of the blessings in my life. With all of the gazes of innocence and discovery from those children, it felt like I was seeing the spirit of my child staring back at me. Some of those children were going to go home to single parent homes and some of them to dual parent homes. Many of them were going home to good homes and some of them to broken homes. To think that I had been participating in something that might have given those children even a small opportunity for discovery and creativity is something that has enormous meaning to me.

It's been said in the Baha'i faith that service to humanity is the ultimate form of prayer. I've always believed that if someone has the means to help someone else then they should help those who need it.

So, maybe the donations and the time working with the H2Orchestra was, in a way, my own way of seeking forgiveness, not just from God but from myself as well.

** ** **

GOD AND LIFE/DEATH

I have always believed that before one puts faith in a higher power, they should at least have a reasonable amount of faith in themselves. Likewise, while it's perhaps easier said than done at times, it's unfair to blame God for a problem or traumatic situation that we, as humans cause.

In my own case, I lost nearly all faith in myself after the abortion. I wasn't about to blame God. I don't think I was ever angry with God after the abortion. I accepted the responsibility of what happened, maybe more than I should have. I not only accepted the responsibility on behalf of myself. I also accepted the responsibility almost on behalf of Anne although Anne and I were equally responsible.

While I believe that most of my anger was directed toward myself and later toward Anne, I maybe felt a little anger toward God. I think for the most part that I just wanted answers. If God wasn't going to come down and allow me the opportunity to trade places with this child, which, of course, He wasn't, I at least wanted to know why I was going through this experience. Why had I been dealt this card? What was the purpose in the grand scheme of things? What kind of man would I become since I obviously would never be the same again? These were some of the questions that I wanted answers to, ...no, I *demanded* answers to.

Nevertheless, when one brings up the topic of God, this also brings up the concept of life after death. For several years I have believed in the Baha'i faith perspective on this matter. That is, to put it simply, our spiritual progress after death is like a "mirror image" of our spiritual progress on earth. In other words, the more selfless we are on earth, the closer to God we will be in the afterlife. Members of the Baha'i faith also believe that the soul of the person who has passed away can still progress in the afterlife as a result of the prayers and selfless acts of those left on earth.

My biggest fear spiritually was that I had been partially responsible for the greatest sin I could imagine-the death of my own child. What right did I have to ask God for forgiveness? Then again, maybe I didn't want forgiveness. I was quite certain that I didn't deserve it. I know that a part of me wanted to suffer for my responsibility. I resigned myself to the fate that I would be spiritually separated from the innocent soul of our child who was killed.

Those times when I simply wanted to fall asleep and wake up in the next life, I felt that I would be closer to my child. Alternatively, I felt that actively ending my own life in one instant would cause me to be very distant from my child in the next life.

If I was seeking spiritual forgiveness at some point, I think that it was not so much in the form of asking. In fact, it was in the form of taking what I had learned and creating something positive out of the negative; treating life in a whole new light. That's the mistake I feel sometimes people make when they pray. That is, asking with out doing something like being of service to another person.

** ** **

COMMITMENT & DETACHMENT

I think that ultimately the abortion was the cause of my breakup with Anne. In fact, I'm quite certain of it. As the weeks after the abortion went by, I felt an increasing amount of resentment toward her. Living a few hours away from her allowed me time to think, perhaps too much time, in fact. This also affected my relationships with others as well as commitment and responsibility in my own life. Needless to say, I swore that I would never meet anyone from the internet ever again.

The thought of loving or trusting someone again was completely out of the question, at least for a while. I didn't date anyone for the longest time. When I did, the attempts failed miserably, usually after the first date. For a while, I had no idea who I was nor did I have an idea of where I was going. I guess I was somewhat of a hermit.

"And it's okay. I'm only running away.
And it's okay. I'm only hiding.
And I'm okay. I only resign myself here.

And it's okay if the candlelight keeps you awake tonight.
And it's okay if it's not me there the next day.
And I'm okay cuz I'm ordinary and I need to fail and lose.

And our life continues limping along.
This is why dignity wears crutches."

Stay Frightened – "The Hermit"

Once I told a counselor I was seeing that "while I had W, X, Y and Z in front of me to complete, I would just work on X and Y and ignore W & Z." Considering my initials, this was an interesting illustration in therapy for me.

When I look back, I am able to identify a personal pattern of inspiration and stagnancy. I would become excited about the possibility of completing a song or section of this book at times. Then the realization of the commitment involved would cause me to become distracted and even overwhelmed. Even daily responsibilities sometimes were among the biggest chores and occasionally went ignored. For example, I might think "why clean the dishes or fill out this job application if it's the weekend and I have money to go buy something?" I guess in some ways I shamefully filled my time with materialistic possessions. Perhaps at the time they were all that I knew to grab a hold of.

I think I've always been somewhat of a late bloomer. I've also been told that I'm basically on my own time frame. However, there is a difference in accomplishing things late and letting things go-accepting the world as "good enough" and succumbing to stagnancy. Occasionally, I would be inspired to look for a new job but then only spend a few hours on a weekend looking. I lost the desire to want something "bad enough." I was *living* but I lost the desire to be *alive*.

** ** **

ON ANNIVERSARIES

Of course the most significant anniversaries since the abortion have been December 4, the day of the conception and January 2, the day of the abortion. The first couple of anniversaries were very difficult as I recall. In the days prior to and on the anniversary dates themselves, I was very isolated and moody. I hadn't really celebrated my birthday with friends and family in at least a few years. It's just another day to me. Besides, how was I supposed to feel that celebrating the day of my birth was okay when the anniversary of my child's death was just the day before?

As the years went on and as my journal writing progressed, the anniversaries were less painful. The second and third year as I recall, I had planned on spending some time alone and perhaps doing some writing, reflecting on the events that happened on that day and how they had transformed me. Instead I felt inclined to be sociable and go hang out with friends. My comfort zone had instructed me to isolate myself and spend those days dwelling on the past and the pain I suffered. However, as time allowed, I became less depressed and didn't think about pushing people away. On those days, I joined the rest of the world. I guess this was a sign that the abortion and my emotions surrounding it got easier to deal with and that the wounds were healing with time.

Anne and I had, at one time, planned to be married in September at the Missouri Botanical Gardens in St. Louis, Missouri. I recall one year I decided to go to the gardens on the anniversary of the date we had planned. This was simply an attempt to draw a conclusion to that chapter of my life, to my relationship with Anne. Coincidentally, the day I went to the gardens, I saw not one, not even two but three wedding parties there. Of course, it's a popular place for weddings. However, I found out that the conclusion wasn't something that was going to be found by entering and exiting a garden. Likewise, I found out that recovery wasn't something I could just do by walking through the garden of life. I was going to have to stare at the demons of guilt, regret and sadness straight in the eyes and hold up a middle finger as they pass.

** ** **

GET OVER IT

People should never listen to those who tell them to "get over it," especially when someone is coping with such a significant loss like the loss of a child. A person can't simply flip a switch and "get over it." Bereavement and sadness aren't limited by time nor is rebirth and progress for that matter. Really, I think what people are trying to say is that one's moodiness or depression is an inconvenience to their good moods.

Not only are people such as these doing their friends a disservice, they are doing their own selves a disservice by not listening to or simply dismissing the pain that the heartbroken person is enduring. They might become acquainted with regret themselves should they find themselves in a similar scenario at some point in their lives.

Fortunately, the friends that I have had have mostly been very good to me. As a result, I didn't have very many people express the "Get over it" attitude. Most everybody understood and respected my space.

After a couple of years had passed, I asked a few close friends as well as my mother if they had any recollection of my behavior during the first few weeks or months following the abortion. I was actually curious to get their perspective. It's kind of like when you are producing an album and you think that you can get the perfect sound doing it all by yourself. I don't think that this is usually the case. You need that additional perspective to understand as much of the full picture as possible.

Some of my friends and my mother as well indicated that the months, and even at times during the first couple of years after the abortion, my moods were shifting up and down more so than they had seen before. They would say that a lot of times I was quieter and less sociable. One friend in particular stated that during our conversations she could hear "the cracks in my voice and the pain in my heart."

Probably the most significant memory that I have regarding talking with my friends immediately after finding out Anne was pregnant was calling a couple of my best friends while crying on the phone and immediately saying "My baby's going to die!" I also remember the dead silence after that. After all, how do you reply to someone who says that to you? This was a good example of the fact that many times one can't solve another's issues with just advice. Sometimes you just need them to be beside you for the ride.

I've always held my friends and family in very high regard. They respected my space when I wanted to be alone and they weren't inconvenienced. I have always been able to count on them if I needed to talk. They were probably much of the reason I didn't go completely insane. Also, one quality which I have most admired about them was that they never really told me something just because they thought that it was what I *wanted* to hear. They always told me what they thought I *should* hear.

It has been said that a person is blessed if they have one best friend during their lifetime. Fortunately, I can honestly say that I have had several very close friends. So, I have always felt very blessed in that regard.

** ** **

"Make friends with the angels, who though invisible are always with you. Often invoke them, constantly praise them, and make good use of their help and assistance in all your temporal and spiritual affairs."

- St. Francis De Sales

** ** **

III

The Letters
2000

Dear Angel,

I was thinking about dreams today. I am often unable to recall my dreams. However, on a rare occasion, I'll have a significant dream and will then be able to recall it vividly.

I'm certain a couple of dreams occurred as a result of my emotions surrounding your demise. One dream that I remember vividly is this:

I found myself in a somewhat plain room. I believe there were only the normal items one might find; a bed, dresser, closet, mirror and window. I was standing on one side of a bed. There was an individual who appeared to be an adult male sitting upright with his feet on the floor. He had short black curly hair. The most significant characteristic, however, was that this person had no arms.

I recall floating around to face this individual. This person appeared to be male, as I said. But even at this point I could not tell for certain. This person, most significantly was without the features of a face. However, I seem to recall a painful feeling as this person may have been attempting to scream.

That's all I remember from that dream.

Thought for the day: You're the most significant dream I'll never forget.

Love,

Me,

*I was reminded of this dream as I read the following passage by author Tom Golden:

William D. Zimmerman

"With the death of a child, for example, the parents are in the belly of grief for years. ....This kind of loss leaves behind the old metaphor for grief which is that of a wound, and brings forth a different image: that of an amputation. Dealing with a loss like the death of a child is more like learning how to live after a part of you has been cut off than it is like healing from a wound."

– Tom Golden from *Swallowed By a Snake*

June 18, 2000

Dearest Angel,

It's a rare occasion that I hear a song or see a film that inspires me and brings me to tears. In fact, it seems as though lately I have had significant trouble becoming inspired. That's just about the scariest feeling for an artist, especially one who is aware of his or her resources having been given for specific purposes.

I saw an incredible film today. It really said so much that I really don't know where to begin. It referred quite a bit to all of the hurt, pain, and hatred that exist in the world today. I think that the main significance in the film was that in spite of such ugliness, miracles can and do exist, even in these conditions. Similarly, you might have been the greatest miracle ever to come into my life. I can't help but feel immense guilt for having been partially responsible for your demise.

Although you're not of this world any longer, you still changed me in ways like a miracle. Even though a part of me died the day you died; the day before my twenty-fifth birthday, I try to remember what really matters in this life: relationships, spending time with people, making others happy and inspiring each other. I'm not perfect. I do fall down from time to time. Yet, in some way, like that movie, you help pull me out of the dark times. This can be a miracle in and of itself.

At one point in the film, the character wondered in spite of laws and his obligations as a death row guard, what he should say to God after questioned why he had let another human being die. I rather wonder the same thing sometimes.

I am sure that you know now, the reasons why your mother made the decision that she did. I hope you know that I set my personal beliefs regarding abortion aside for her. I was going to support her no matter what. I want you to know that you were conceived in love. I've spoken about how I would have traded places with you if I knew you would have grown up healthy. I meant that.

Lastly, today is Father's Day. I called my father to wish him a good day. I wonder if you thought of me today. God knows you never leave me. I believe that I'll always be your Daddy, even now. Tell me, angel, once we pass on, do we still dream? I love you. Be well, angel.

Love,

Me (Dad)

July-Aug. 2000

Dearest Angel,

I was thinking recently about an event that occurred a few weeks ago. I'm going to initialize the names of the people involved just in case this journal reaches the stage of publication. I went over to J. & D.'s apartment. They informed me that our friends S. & K. just had their baby and we were off to the hospital to visit. I guess it didn't really occur to me where we were going until we arrived. I mean, I knew we would be walking through the maternity ward but, moreover, I was to walk through a place similar to the one you would have been born in. It was a somewhat unpleasant experience. However, I didn't perceive it to be a respectable idea for me to wait outside.

When we arrived on the appropriate floor, I saw much of the similar equipment that I might have seen if you'd have been born; the beds in which the babies are placed with their name tags on the back, the incubators and other things. One item of interest was this. Along the main hallway where the patient rooms were located were the inked footprints of many, if not all of the babies who were brought into the world at this hospital. There were different colors of ink for the prints and many different names. I couldn't help but picture your footprint up there on the wall with your name written just below it. That's all for now.

All my love,

Me

July-Aug., 2000

Dearest Angel,

I was watching television today and a woman was recalling an incident with her one-year old child. She stated that she was looking at her child who at that moment had a huge smile on his or her face. The child was looking over its mother's shoulder though. She asked if the child was looking at an angel. The child nodded, "Yes." The woman stated that she believed children could see angels better than adults. So that makes me wonder-where you're at now...do you see angels? Are you among them?

Love Always,

Me.

"Perhaps children's innocence, wherever it comes from, contributes to the fact that they seem to see angels more often."

- John Ronner

No date, 2000

Dear Angel,

I had another "interesting" dream two nights ago. I remember walking uphill toward this house. I recall my reasoning for approaching this house was to find out about a child. It was rather vague. Strangely, I did not recognize the two people who answered the door. In the dream it seemed that I thought I had a child or might have one.

One of the people at the door quoted a name for the mother. Oddly, it wasn't the name of your mother, which I would have expected to hear. They said that she had gone. They also said that she had given birth to a baby boy. The last thing that happened was that I turned away and started crying. Then I woke up.

Until next time,

Daddy

P.S. I later wondered if the inclined path I took in the dream was symbolic. Perhaps it represented the upward climb I must take to finding out who I am and what happened to me as a result of your demise.

P.S.2 I also wondered if someone or something used the dream to let me know what gender you would have been. Was that *your* way of letting me know?

William D. Zimmerman

October 14, 2000

Dear Angel,

As I may have told you before, I usually don't remember my dreams. However, I've been having some reasonably disturbing dreams as of late. Please ask God to help make them stop.

Yours Sincerely,

Me

October 14, 2000(2nd Entry)

Dearest Angel,

A couple of days ago I made a photocopy of the image of the drawing which your mother made of her sonogram. I made a couple of photocopies, actually. One of these I placed above the doorway inside my room facing east. I did this to serve as a simple reminder that you're probably watching me from somewhere and that I should not be concerned with worldly desires so much. You know what though? It's rather symbolic. That is, your image above my doorway. It's symbolic because you'll always be in my heart through every transition, corridor or doorway of life.

Love Forever,

Daddy

October 17, 2000

Dearest Angel,

I found myself failing yet again today – not refusing vain imaginations. I feel so desperate, so lost sometimes. As a matter of fact, I think that my subconscious mind had told me, in some ways that it didn't care. That scared the hell out of me, really. I should be so thankful right now. I'm helping to promote a record label. I have all of these resources but I am not using them to their full potential. In fact, I often take them for granted. Why? They're here for a purpose, just as your passing, while tragic, had its reasons. You're influencing a lot of my art and hopefully people will gain a positive reaction from my songs – a sense of understanding perhaps.

Anyway, I'll never succeed taking things for granted. Please don't ever leave me. You know, I found myself in the shower hunching down with my head in my hands and the water pouring over me. For whatever reason, the water seemed to have gotten noticeably colder. I imagined rain or tears from heaven and you watching above.

Yours Sincerely (trying once again, today)

Me.

December 5, 2000

Dear Angel,

It should come as no surprise to you that I was thinking about you today. Of course, I think of you every day. However, today is a special occasion, you see. Today would have been the day you were conceived. I still recall every part of that weekend just like it was yesterday. I remember the sparkles on your mother's face. She had this walk-in closet where we slept. I remember the CD that played on repeat throughout the night and into the morning. It was "Darkest Days" by Stabbing Westward. What an ironic title considering the darkness of the days which passed after your demise. Your mother had these plastic glow-in-the-dark stars all around this walk-in closet where we slept. This brings to mind an idea I had. Why is it that so often, people point upward to heaven?

Isn't God all around us? I mean, I know you're around from time to time. I've felt your presence. You're with me today.

Love Forever,

Daddy

December 12, 2000

Dear Angel,

I was at the grocery store a couple of nights ago. I passed by the magazine rack and noticed a parenting related magazine. On the cover was a child-perhaps about two or three years old I guess. She had a pair of golden wings on her back.

What color are your wings?

Love,

Me

The Letters
2001

Dear Angel,

Well, today marks the two-year anniversary of the day you left us. I guess it's more appropriate to say it's the day your mother removed you. She removed you from her womb but not from our lives. You are a part of our lives forever. Why do I get the feeling that she wants to forget about everything? I think she wants to forget about us. I suppose that's not fair to assume such a thing because I don't speak to her any more. Then again, perhaps that's part of the very reason she wants to forget. I guess it's a bit arrogant of me to assume her feelings. I thought it was a safe bet as she had the Tarot CD for about a week and she hadn't listened to my song, "The Lovers" yet.*

Anyway, today isn't about her and me. It's about remembering you. You know, I still have several answering machine messages that she left me. They're recorded onto a cassette tape. They span the time from when we met initially until probably near the end of our relationship. I even have the message that she left after she had found out that she was pregnant with you. I'll never forget that day. We had already discussed what would happen in the event she did become pregnant. However, I was going to support her in whatever she decided. I didn't want her to have to deal with any more pressure than she already had to deal with. After all, I was her first. Your mother was strong though.

What would have happened if I had spoken about my feelings against abortion and the importance of your life? Do you think she would have given you up for adoption? She said we wouldn't have been able to give you a good life. However, I think even I would have made it work if put into that situation though.

I forced myself to watch a film on television about abortion. I don't know why. I think, perhaps it was that I wanted to better understand what your mother went through. The method they used in the film was vacuum-the same method that was used to extract you.

Why did she have to select the day before my birthday? I often wonder if her subconscious mind told her in a vengeful manner that would be a good day. While I doubt that is a realistic situation, the thought has crossed my mind.

Yes, my birthday is tomorrow. Why do I feel old? I don't celebrate my birthday with family or friends anymore, really. I don't even want so much as a "Happy Birthday." Well, how can it be that happy if a part of me died the day before? I do appreciate their thoughts though.

You know, as mentally estranged as I felt after your demise, one thing I knew for certain is that I would have taken your place. I believe I was prepared to trade everything in this life of mine, make my Will and Testament and exit this world. After all, it wasn't fair that you weren't given a chance. Perhaps you could have affected more lives in a positive manner than I. I just hope that, through the resources I've been blessed with that a few people will be affected in an uplifting way-either through this book or through one of my songs. That's really the best feeling-the most humbling feeling, in fact; that I can take lessons learned from a negative situation and turn them into a positive situation.

Love Always,

Me

* The "Tarot" CD to which this line refers is in fact a CD called "The Power of a New Aeon: Musical Impressions of the Tarot." This CD was put out by Palace of Worms Records and features my song "The Lovers" as well as "The Hermit" by Stay Frightened which I quote in this book.

January 22, 2001

Dear Angel,

A very strange thing happened today. I went into the living room to speak to my housemate about the recording session that I had with Jeff and Rebecca yesterday. So, we talked briefly about it. By the way, this was approximately 9:45 AM. My housemate asked about a noise he heard about 45 minutes prior to our conversation. I hadn't heard anything as I was either asleep or had just woken up at the time he told me he heard the sounds, which were like those of a baby crying.

He said they'd start, stop and this repeated a couple of times. I thought this was extremely weird since I didn't have my CD player, radio or computer on as I so often do. He said he wasn't dreaming and that he remembers hearing it after returning from the bathroom. I would also like to note that we don't live in the near vicinity of any babies or small children.

I later sat down to eat my lunch I turned the TV on but couldn't find anything that caught my interest. So I settled on a cable news channel which is normally the last resort for me. My mouth dropped when I learned what event had its anniversary today. I learned that today was the anniversary of Roe vs. Wade – the very famous court case in which abortion was made legal here in the US. How strange to hear about such "noises" on a day like today.

Why would my housemate hear them and not me? I could understand why he'd hear them especially if I was indeed, asleep. We have been friends for over a decade. I do believe in kindred spirits. I do believe that what affects a person can also affect those close to that person.

79

But I might have been awake though I doubt it. Anyway, what could it have been? Anything? Does something want to punish me? Are you always trying to reach me? Do you forgive me?

Love Always,

Me

.

February, 7, 2001

Dearest Angel,

Yet another strange dream last night. I found us in a pool filled with water. I seem to recall other parents and children in there as well. It seemed as though we were all teaching our children how to swim. The strange element of the dream was that I had almost assumed that it was natural for you to swim and not drown. Upon realizing this was not so, that you would drown, I picked you up and held you near the level of the water in effort to teach you to swim.

The next thing I recall was you facing me in the pool approximately a few feet away. I watched as you sank into the water. The strange part about this scene was the expression on your face. You weren't sad or angry or crying for help. In fact, there was a look of contentment about your face. It was rather disturbing.

I often wonder if you're trying to reach me and tell me something from beyond. If so, what am I supposed to know?

Yours,

Me.

P.S. Rather than teaching you to swim, I think perhaps you are teaching me to progress.

March 1, 2001

Dearest Angel,

Another bad dream last night. Actually, it wasn't so much the dream that disturbed me. Rather, it was how I felt as I was waking up. I don't know whether it's fortunate or not with regard to the fact that I can't recall that much of it. I recall a profound sense of nurturing. I was the one who was providing you with love and care. I was an extraordinarily proud father in this dream. One scene impacted me in particular.

I was walking into a room to check on you. You were in a car seat which was underneath a blanket on a bed-much like I was for a good portion of this past week. Anyway, I recall lifting the cover to check on you as if it was normal for you to be under the cover. I walked away thinking you were alright. As I stated earlier, it wasn't so much the dream that upset me as it was the slow and painful drift back into reality of waking up. I awoke to a profound sense of loss. Sometimes I'd with I wouldn't wake up from feelings like those of this dream I spoke of. As least I might feel more complete near you.

Sometimes I think dreams may be curses. In some ways they can be positive tools for learning. Perhaps they can provide revelations for us. Yet, in my case-or in cases such as mine I should say, perhaps the profound sense of longing and loss is a result of nightmares and dreams. Maybe they are like lessons or punishment in teaching me to progress, to work on things that truly matter in this world or to not be lethargic. Like I said, there have been days in the past couple of years where I wished I wouldn't wake from my dreams. But the fundamental line is this. There is a purpose to everything. I have a purpose to fulfill as well. Inasmuch as your loss was very painful to me, there is also a purpose behind me writing this to you. I hope it can affect someone else someday.

Sincerely,

Daddy

March 3, 2001

Dearest Angel,

Two days ago, you were watching over me, weren't you? It was the last day of the intercalary days – the few days before the new calendar starts in the Baha'i faith. These are days normally devoted to visiting the sick as well as gift-giving and the like. I was contemplating donating some stuffed animals to an office of the Illinois Police Department as I had done a couple of years ago. During situations of domestic abuse and other traumatic situations, the officers often give these to the children involved in effort to comfort them.

I had been thinking about my debts and how I need to save money-somewhat selfish I suppose. Then I started thinking about you and how you were never given a chance. It felt only natural that I should go buy some stuffed animals to donate. If they can provide some little girl or boy with even a temporary sense of comfort, then it was worthwhile. I also didn't want it to be a one-time thing that I did.

Sometimes it's like I can feel you looking down upon me, watching over me. I think you were that day, reminding me again what really matters in this life; compassion, relationships and love.

You might be aware that I've been working on a song called "Halo of Snowflakes." It's about you, having been conceived in the winter and how you are still watching over me.

As I went to deliver the stuffed animals, I was thinking about just that-you looking over me. Strangely enough as thinking about this nearly brought tears to my eyes, it began to rain.

Love Always,

Me

May 13, 2001

Dearest Angel,

I apologize for not having written in some time. Today is a holiday-Mother's Day. It's a day for us to honor our mothers and all they have done for us. I wonder if your mother is thinking of you today. I wonder if you're watching over her.

Yours Truly,

Daddy

September 20, 2001

Dear Angel,

Once again, I apologize for not having written in quite some time. The past week has been unreal. Some evil people-some terrorists attacked the United States. Two terrorists crashed planes into the towers of the World Trade Center in New York City. Another plane crashed into the Pentagon and another in a rural area in Pennsylvania. Thousands of people have died or are missing. Why another human being would do something like this is inconceivable.

It's very surreal to see what you know will be regarded as such a historical event. I can't imagine what the people who were there were thinking when they saw the towers fall. What I really can't imagine is how it must feel to be the person on the other end of the phone speaking to the person who's calling from the plane. How can you summarize all that you want to say within minutes or even seconds before your loved one dies?

Undoubtedly I think I'm going to remember this day for the rest of my life. I'll even remember the color of the shirt I was wearing when I heard the news. It was white.

Other than these initial thoughts, words escape me when I think about what has happened only a few days ago. So, I guess that's all for now. Until then....

All My Love,

Daddy

September 26, 2001

Dearest Angel,

As you may know, I've been working for this place doing customer service for a number of clients via phone, chat and email. One of the clients sells quite a few costumes, especially since it's getting close to Halloween. The hot items this year are these adorable costumes for infants & toddlers. Many of the costumes are animals like sheep, butterflies, ladybugs, pigs or skunks. I can't help but imagine taking you out Trick or Treating your first time. Thought for the week: I'm certain you're dressed in an angel's outfit all the time.

Always,

Daddy

No Date, Sept, 2001

Dear Angel,

I'm very aware you're with me always. Life here is often...
well, difficult at best. I'd give anything to have you back here.
One thing-perhaps the only thing that motivates me is you and
knowing I'll be with you again someday. I've put your mother's
drawing of you above my doorway. I also put some Christmas
lights around it. But in spite of all of this, why do I slip and fall
every now and then? Deep down inside I keep you in mind at
all times. Missing you, severely.
    Wish you were here.

Daddy

October 17, 2001

Dear Angel,

Winter is fast approaching and I feel closer to you – my child of the snow. As you may know, I've been taking some anti-depressant medication as well as seeing a counselor to try and work out some issues I've been dealing with the past few years. My counselor, Charlie made some good points when he stated (and I readily admitted) that living in past events is going to do nothing to change them. That's true though it's easier said than done. It seems, for the most part, I've lived that way for a while now.

A significant thought came to mind recently though. I'm not sure I want to let you go. It seems like if I don't forgive myself for having been responsible for your demise, then I'll remain closer to you. Likewise, I feel like if I forgive myself and try to peel some of my guilt away, then I'll feel farther away and I don't want to feel that. I really don't know what to do at this point. Can you guide me?

I wanted to mention one other thing. I found a little piece of nostalgia while cleaning out one of my closets yesterday. It was a crystal heart that your mother gave me one time when I went to visit her in Kansas. It was a reference to something I said to her in the chat room I met her in. I had made an indication of action to "serve my heart to her on a crystal plate." For a moment it brought back some memories.

Anyway, I guess this is a good closing point. I'm thinking of you always. Your grandpa will be here shortly.

Love Always,

Daddy

October 24, 2001

Dearest Angel,

Well, I guess you're aware that heaven gained an angel and you gained a family member's company today. My grandmother (your great-grandmother) on my dad's side died today. She was in her early 90s. She passed away peacefully so that's somewhat comforting.

I'm feeling a significant amount of guilt right now – mostly in two respects. I feel I should have expressed more appreciation for her financial gifts during the holidays. There's no question about that. She's one of the main reasons I was able to buy some of the musical equipment. Her gifts allowed me to take care of other things needed.

I also feel bad for my father right now. After he drove back to the east coast from Illinois, he went to visit his mother in the hospital only to find her not there. It turns out that he had just missed her by a few hours. So, I can't imagine what he's feeling right now.

Anyway, you've got some family up there. Give them my love.

Forever Yours,

Daddy

November 22, 2001

Dear Angel,

Well, today is Thanksgiving-a holiday where we're supposed to be humbled and thankful for the things in our lives. I don't normally find myself in the degree of holiday spirit like most people. However, today I feel humble and grateful for the things in my life.

I've got a wonderful mother & father, a great family, a job, a roof over my head and some wonderful friends. What more could I ask for? Answer: You. In the same breath of gratitude today, there is the sigh of regret and guilt that you're not here in the flesh. I know you're always here in spirit though. I'm forever grateful for the inspiration and the joys of life-things that you've taught me. Though words will never be enough, perhaps I can show my thanks to you in how I live my life.

Thank You. I love you and will continue to carry you throughout my life.

Always,

Daddy

November 26, 2001

Dearest Angel,

I often wonder why people look at someone's exterior and judge them upon that impression. For example, why do people look at me strange because I dress mostly in black and I have long hair? Why are people so quick to assume? I try to be a good spiritual person. I make an effort to serve humanity.

I know that if you were here you'd look at me and hopefully love me without condition! While I'm not a daddy in the real world, I hope that I can serve humanity in such a way that I can live with you in mind. If you're not with me in person, you'll be with me in thought and in my good deeds.

Love Always,

Daddy

December 3, 2001

Dearest Angel,

I heard something on the radio coming home from work the other day which I found nearly unbelievable. There was a news report of a man who had laced some Kool-Aid with insecticide and gave it to his pregnant girlfriend. He did this in effort to make his girlfriend have a miscarriage. I heard this and wanted to cry. What kind of mind could do something like this? How could someone be so selfish? Who wants to live in a world with people like this in it?

I love you,

Daddy

December 4, 2001

Dear Angel,

I can recall the sparkles in her face and the glow-in-the-dark stars on the walls just like it was yesterday. I can still hear the music playing in the background continuously.

I guess I don't have to tell you what day it is today. It was two years ago today when your conception occurred. Actually, it was sometime between the 4th and the 5th of December when you came into existence. I never thought that night would change my life forever. In more ways than not, I feel regrets for my responsibility that night and the fact that I also changed the life of a girl in her early twenties.

I would never in eternity go so far as to say that "some good" came out of that night. However, inasmuch as I may stumble and fall on occasion, I'm trying to carry you with me in every day of my life. Essentially, while the hole in my heart may never be repaired, I can do the most I can to turn the negativity from having gone through your demise into positive actions.

Unsigned

December 26, 2001

Dear Angel,

What's heaven really like? Is it a physical place where we go when we die or is it more of a psychological place for which we are partially responsible? Is it all around us in every facet of life; the good deeds we perform, the beauty we see in the eyes of someone we care for or the feeling of a presence of someone who's passed away? Can the soul really progress after death? Is it possible to see loved ones after we die or is that idea a product of humanity's wishful thinking? Do angels really have wings?

Unsigned.

The Letters
2002

January 1, 2002

Dear Angel,

And so we begin another year. Let's hope this one is better than last year. Happy New Year, angel.

Love,

Me

January 2, 2002

Dear Angel,

I suppose I don't have to tell you what anniversary today is. Of course, it was three years ago today when you were given back unto heaven. I can almost recall that day as though it was yesterday. While the emptiness hasn't healed, nor will it ever completely, I've been trying to keep you in mind everyday when I communicate with people.

You know sometimes memory can be a gift and other times, a curse. While the curse of memory can put the hole right back in our heart, the gift of memory can allow us to learn from our mistakes and remember the positive things in life.

I wonder a lot about if your mother thinks about you often, such as on a day like today. You know, I recently asked her for a copy of the letter that she wrote to you a long time ago. To my surprise, she actually acknowledged my request and said she'd copy it and mail me a copy if she could locate the original. I'll be more surprised if she does that.

Well, I guess that's all that I can think of right now. Know that not a minute goes by without me thinking about you. I love you now and forever.

Always,

Daddy

January 29, 2002

Dearest Angel,

One thing I've tried to learn from my counselor is to try to do new things or "try on new glasses" as he would say. As I get older I find myself doing this a bit more often than normal.

You know, one of my most favorite things to do is making people laugh either by making a joke or just with my sarcastic humor in general. A number of people over the years have suggested that I try to get involved in stand-up comedy. Earlier this month I tried to do just that. When all was said and done, I think it was successful on the two occasions I did try it.

One of the greatest things anyone can achieve is the ability to make someone laugh or even smile. I've always said that there's a purpose to every relationship whether it's a life-long commitment or just in making someone smile.

Perhaps it's a combination of two things that makes me more aware of this as I get older. Of course, one of the things is having kept you in mind the last three years. I think the second thing that makes me keep this in mind is the fact that I'm getting older and as a result, time is of the essence.

That's all for now. I hope all is well wherever you are.

Sincerely,

Me

January 31, 2002

Dearest Angel,

I have been reading a book lately on the subject of synesthesia; a psychological condition that occurs in different forms. Generally speaking, though, this occurs when one sense is triggered by an initial sensory reaction. So, someone might see a certain type of tree and have an overwhelming particular smell. Likewise, someone could be eating a particular type of food and notice particular shapes in the taste.

You know, I've always thought that it was possible to paint someone's portrait with music or to describe abstract and intangible things with the feeling through sound.

This principle though brings several questions to my mind. For example, why is anger always associated with red? Also, why is blue associated with sadness or depression? More than that though, it makes me wonder, "What's the color of loss or sorrow and how would you paint it with sound?" Also what are the shapes of these concepts?

Moreover, what color is Heaven? How can one, through music, convey the feeling of what those people may look like after we die or the feeling of their nearby presence? Often I wonder if the melodies or polyphonies that I hear all the time in my head come from you.

Anyway, I guess that's all at this time.

Forever Yours,

Daddy.

March 12, 2002

Dearest Angel,

Once again, I realize that it's been some time since I've written and again I apologize. There's been quite a lot going on during the last month and a half.

I figured today would be a good day to write. Yesterday was the 6 month anniversary of the terrorist attacks on America. It was one of those situations where you never forget where you were when you heard the news. Though in a more personal level, I recall right where I was when I lost you.

You know, it's true how a simple act of recalling an incident can put either the feelings of emptiness or even joy right back in to one's heart almost as if it was yesterday. Another thing, why is it that we as humans have to deal with tragedy in order to appreciate the gifts we are given. Is it with the purpose that we appreciate what we do have and what we do accomplish? A phrase that comes to mind is "heaven knows." Well, does heaven know? Do you know?

Inasmuch as I may have progressed in the last 4 years, there's been this over-riding sense of some negative force trying to hold me back. In the same breath perhaps I've never given myself enough credit for the things I have accomplished over the last few years. As an artist, I know that we humans can often be our own worst critics. It's much easier to focus on the negative than on the positive things in our lives. Does that make sense?

I know in the past few letters, I've told you about some of the more positive things that have happened in the recent months. I think that we've reached a point in this project where I can perhaps start to focus on the many positive events or situations that have happened since I've started trying to heal from, or at least deal with your loss. Before we get to that though, I need to tell you about a very low point that I reached a little while ago.

It was just before Valentine's Day. I was excited about a possible relationship with this girl I met from St. Louis. While we shared quite an amount of things in common, things spiraled at really an alarming rate and before I knew it, I found myself experiencing patterns of old relationships. By that I mean trying to "mold" this person into my ideal soul mate though I truthfully know that this person could never be that. Another characteristic was "falling" too fast and too soon in the relationship.

You're probably wondering how this relates to my relationship with you. One thing I've noticed is this; it's only been in recent years that I've become increasingly aware of my actions and open to the possibilities for the reasons behind them.

Back to the "low" point that I was telling you about. After noticing reoccurring patterns with my emotions running rampant in this new relationship, qualities that I was certain I grew out of years ago, a typical "floodgate" had opened and I came down really hard. Although, I'm not entirely sure why, I wanted to punish myself for having taken what seemed like a major step back.

I didn't eat properly for a couple of days. I also took this amethyst that the aforementioned person gave me and made 3 vertical marks on my left wrist. I don't think I actually wanted to die and I don't think that the issue with the friend was the main problem. I think there was a greater issue at hand. I think that I just wanted to see how much physical pain I could endure without actually going over the edge. Of course, as I've told you, there've been moments when I got so depressed after losing you where I wouldn't have minded if I went to sleep and didn't wake up. However, that's entirely different from voluntarily giving up. I've always viewed suicide as the most cowardly and selfish act. I could never put friends and relatives through that.

Anyway, I wanted to tell you that as it leads into a really positive experience. At a very low point, I phoned a friend whom I knew had turned her life around being involved in a meditative energy healing practice called Reiki. I won't go into detail but I tell you, after we were done I felt incredibly different. It's definitely something I would like to pursue.

During our time together though, something rather frightening occurred. At one point, my friend ended the Reiki session with me because she had seen or felt some entity-a very negative one. I felt this in a dream a couple of nights later.

Well, that's all for now. We'll talk again soon I'm sure.

All My Love,

Daddy

March 14, 2002

Dearest Angel,

I'm sorry for the long delay in sending this. Anyway, I'm coming back, so to speak. A new transition is about to begin-new surroundings, a new beginning.

As Always,

Me

March 28, 2002

Dearest Angel,

Well, I've finally made it into my new apartment. It was very uncomfortable at first. I guess that's to be expected when you're used to being in the same location for nearly three years. But with new surroundings and new people come new inspiration and that's precisely what I need at this point regardless of how uncomfortable it may feel at first.

As you know Angel, I've been feeling rather stagnant and uninspired for the past few months. I've felt like this book and my venture into comedy was predominantly what I was supposed to be doing. I think that perhaps I was subconsciously waiting for this recent transition.

I want you to know that one of the first things I took into my apartment was a photocopy of your picture, which I placed upon the windowsill of the back bedroom. At this point, the rooms look pretty plain with no posters hanging on the walls and numerous boxes scattered about the floors.

I know that I acquired this apartment for some specific reason. My mother actually stumbled upon it by accident. It was like a godsend I think - even in a wonderful neighborhood.

Why can transitions often be so difficult? Aside from the discomfort of being in a new environment, I was upset about leaving the old. In addition, I felt like I didn't deserve the things that people are giving me for my apartment.

I think that there's some strange connection between this "hole" that seems to have grown since you died and the space that manifests itself when I feel like I'm undeserving. But these questions remain: What is the definition of the "thing" that's supposed to occupy this hole or holes? Where did it begin and how? Where did it go and how do I put it back?

I know without a doubt that things overall are getting better for me. I almost feel like with this new beginning, we are nearing the end of this section of the book. Then again, I guess I should let you know what it's like to be moving forward through the first part of this next "chapter," so to speak. By the way, on the first night alone at my new apartment, I turned on the radio and sat down to eat. The first song I heard had the words "I'm moving on." Is there a difference between moving "on" and moving "forward?"

I think I prefer to say that I'm moving forward. At least that seems to be a better choice for a word when one wants to imply progress. Nevertheless, I thought this line from the song I heard was rather symbolic.

Well, I'm drawing a blank at this time. So, if I think of anything else, I'll make an appendix and write it in later.

Yours "moving forward,"

Me

May 4, 2002

Dearest Angel,

I witnessed something the other day which I wanted to tell you about. I accompanied a very good friend to a basketball game in which his daughter was playing.

It wasn't just a good basketball game that I was watching. I had known for some time that, for whatever reason, I was emotionally attached to the concept of succeeding through tension or finding a way out of difficult situations. I'm still unsure as to whether I had always enjoyed putting myself in such situations. That remains to be seen.

The game was also about children doing something they love. There during one of the quarter breaks, was a young boy shooting baskets by himself. My friend had made a good point when he, in reference to the boy said the following; 'That's what it's all about," he said. "...the American dream, just a kid, a basketball and a hoop." He's exactly correct. What more could be said about that?

Well, that's all I can think to write about right now. I just wanted to let you know what I had seen. Be well, angel.

With love,

Daddy

May 5, 2002

Dearest Angel,

I did something the other day which I wanted to tell you about. I do want to mention beforehand though, I'm not telling you this to sound arrogant. We have reached the point in the book where the focus is more geared toward living moving forward and turning the negative into the positive.

Anyway, my friend and I had gone to Einstein's Bagels to eat. Since we were there at closing time, one of the employees asked us if we wanted to take home some of the bagels that they were going to throw away. Thinking that they were going to give us a small bag with just a few bagels, we said, "Sure." After they set down two half-filled trash bags, we must have had over 250 bagels-more than enough to feed quite a few homeless people.

So after my friend and I gave away several bags to friends, relatives, my landlord and maintenance guy, I took the last few bags of bagels and a case of Dr. Pepper and gave them to some homeless people standing outside a shelter in downtown St. Louis. It just occurred to me to do this while I was coming home from a nightclub last Monday. I don't know if they'll all get eaten but hopefully some do. It'wells situations such as this which make me think you're somewhere watching over me reminding me what really matters in this life.

That's all for now. I'll talk to you soon.

Love Always,

Daddy

May 9, 2002

Dearest Angel,

I'm just going to spill this one out from the heart and not "think" too much before writing the words down.

I'm quite certain that yesterday was a pivotal point in my mental growth and therefore, a critical point in the book. All throughout the book, there carries an underlying theme, somewhat regarding a "missing piece" that's been inside of me at least for the past year, perhaps to a lesser extent in the previous couple of years. It was something more than just the sense of having lost you.

I couldn't draw closure to this chapter-this book until I was able to put a "name" to this "thing." Well, it's come to my attention recently what this "thing" is – Passion. That's passion for life, love, art and progress in my personal life.

I have been able to put this name to the missing piece, I believe mostly thanks to a relationship with a wonderful soul whom I met nearly three weeks ago. Just having spoken to her for hours and being in her presence has made me feel more alive and open to newer possibilities and avenues as well as not being so anal or limiting on what I do or just how I think.

But of course I'll move slowly as nothing is for certain and quite honestly it's hard for me to trust or think of loving someone again for a while. I still love you though.

Always,

Dad

May 11, 2002

Dearest Angel,

Hello, I hope that you are well. This will most likely be the final "letter" in this book which will bring closure to this chapter of my life.

I'm writing this to you from a hospital in Ohio. It is at an institution such as this where life begins and ends. Two floors above is the maternity ward where children are brought into the world. Just today as I was talking on the phone in the lobby, I saw a brand new mother carrying her baby home. However, all around are people on the decline as well.

It's both distressing and inspiring at the same time. It's distressing in the sense of witnessing people in the hallways who appear to be near the point of dying. It's inspiring though, to walk away with the sense of an appreciation for life and how we should treat one another well. It's also inspirational to witness the compassion from the hospital staff in how the patients here are cared for. Everyone seems loving and compassionate.

I used to wonder often if it would bring any closure to me if I gave you a name. I was speaking to a friend via telephone some time ago. She had told me about how she named and baptized her child that she had aborted some time earlier. She also spoke about the closure it brought to her and the peace of mind necessary to progress through life. I also recall picking up books in the bookstore and reading about how women in Asia who'd had miscarriages or even abortions and how they'd perform what they called a naming ritual.

And so, with this having been kept in mind, I think that there's this one last loose end that needs to be tied. I say that on the chance that you're somewhere either waiting for me to draw some closure to this chapter so that you may progress in the next life or that I may move forward in my own life. Well, with this said, I give you your name Winter.

Be well, Winter.

Always, Me

William D. Zimmerman

A Letter to Your Mother

Dear "Anne,"

I'm not even really certain as to where to begin. I have such a wide array of thoughts and emotions regarding the short history you and I shared and the many moments in between those days and the present. Obviously, the most significant memory is the situation surrounding the abortion.

We could say the primary focus of this letter is to make it clear to myself about how I felt about you with regard to the abortion. It's not so much that I want you to know what I went through. You probably won't ever know that this book is even out, much less read it.

I have often wondered how the abortion has affected you, especially since we stopped speaking in April of 1999. I have often wondered if you had bad dreams as I have, if you have spent as much time wondering about the things that might have been and how our lives would have been different had you not gone through with the abortion. I wondered if you spent hours pouring your heart out to your friends. I wondered if you reached the point when you weren't really sure if your own life was worth living. Also, I wonder if you have thought about how we would have dealt with the situation together if we were still in a relationship.

Nevertheless, at this point, I'm writing this mainly for the following reasons:

1. To make sense of my feelings about you in relation to the abortion and the months after. That is, to organize, document and purge as much of the negative or unhealthy emotions as possible. Yeah, I know that probably sounds selfish but oh well. I think I deserve to be somewhat selfish. After all, it was you whose interests I was looking out for back then. 2. I think that it's important for my readers to understand how I have felt about our relationship over the past few years. 3. Additionally, (and

to a much lesser extent) if you ever pick up this book after it's published you will know how I felt and perhaps why I didn't disclose my emotions during the time that we were together. The easiest emotion, I think one can feel as a result of a situation of this magnitude is anger. So, let's go ahead and begin with that one. There's a part of me that wanted to lash out at you for what you did. I'm noticing now that the ink from this pen is making deeper lines with my pressing down on the page as I think about the abortion and my feelings toward you regarding it. You took away a piece of me-a piece that I can never get back. Sure, it's possible that I may have children sometime in the future but this one would have been the first and it cannot be brought back. As a result, an enormous gaping emotional hole was left inside of me, one that will never completely heal.

Perhaps I'm living in the past. Perhaps I'm past trying to hold onto the element of hope-hope for a child of my own one day. Nevertheless, I recall you never asked me if I thought you should keep the child, abort it or give it up for adoption. You know, I've sometimes even wondered if you were *waiting* for me to say something or stand up for the baby.

I'm sure you'd recall the conversation that you and I had regarding what may happen in the event you did get pregnant. How ironic was it that we had that conversation on the very weekend when the conception occurred.

You stated that you "were not ready to be a mommy" and I was not "ready to be a daddy." That's almost like saying that the child arrived at an inconvenient moment in our lives. Also, it's one thing for you to say that you weren't ready to be a mother but what makes you think that I wasn't ready to be a father? You said that the child would grow up with your parents taking primary care of him or her and that would not be a good life. Well, at least it would have been a life. Also, what makes you think that the baby would automatically live with your family? Why couldn't you have given birth and then signed over all rights to me? I would have found a way to support the child.

And what gave you the right to decide that I "wasn't ready to be a daddy?" The fact is that I would have been, ready or not.

Here's another thing. Why the hell did you have the operation the day before my twenty-fifth birthday? Did you want to keep this situation imprinted in my mind as much as possible (as if it wouldn't have been had you chosen another day) or was it just convenient to have the abortion on the first Saturday which you could get an appointment?

I think what I find to be most confusing about this is the fact that, during the days leading up to the abortion, you spoke of yourself and the child in such a nurturing manner. "The baby and I are going to lie down in front of the speakers and listen to Daddy's tape," you said. What about when you just used the word "we" while you were talking about what you were going to eat or do that day? How could you seem so caring and nurturing and yet go through with the abortion? Was the child too young or too small to be "real" enough for you? Well, it was real to me. The drawing you made of the sonogram after 3 ½ weeks added to the reality and the gravity of the situation for me.

In spite of the anger I'm inclined to feel toward you about your decision to abort, there's also a sense of sympathy. I could never imagine how difficult this situation-the decision, operation and psychological & emotional aftermath has been for you.

I once forced myself to watch a film on cable television about abortion. It was set in a clinic that performed abortions in the same manner as you had. I think some part of me wanted to try to endure some of the pain that you felt even if I could only feel a fraction of it by viewing this film. I also wanted to better understand what you went through. That's exactly why I asked you if you still had a copy of the letter that you wrote to our little angel. I only have, copied on my hard drive, some segments of some of the poetry you wrote in the chat room where we met. Like I said, I just wanted to understand better. I would have been there with you at the doctor's office when you found out you were pregnant if I didn't think that I would be risking my own life on the treacherous snow and ice-covered highways.

In some ways, however, I feel like I owe you a little gratitude. It was because of the drawing of the sonogram that you made and copied for me, that I was able to realize more clearly the reality and the gravity of the situation. That drawing has helped me to realize that certain things are more important in life and that people, life and relationships shouldn't be taken for granted. In a way, though, this book would never have been written nor could a number of people be helped if it wasn't for you.

Maybe I also owe you a bit of thanks for being the strong one after we split up? At least it seemed as though you were the strong one. When I thought that I had made a mistake and wanted to maybe work things out, when I was ready to pack up all my things and move out to Kansas, you said that you couldn't bounce back that easily and that I needed to find "the one." In retrospect, moving out there wouldn't have been the best decision so I'm sort of glad that you were not willing to "bounce back" so easily after we split.

Perhaps you never knew how much I cared about you or about the baby. Perhaps society had also taught me to shelter my feelings. Maybe you would have seen how much I cared about you and life in general had I shown my true feelings about the abortion. Maybe we'd still be together because of that. My initial reaction was to support you regardless.

We were kids it seems. I know that I have grown up quite a bit in the past few years. I sometimes wonder how you've been and how the abortion has affected your life and how you treat others.

I wonder if the news of this book will reach you when it's finally published. I wonder if you'll be browsing through a book store some day and come across it. Nevertheless, I don't look back too much anymore. It's all forward from here. I hope your life is met with health, happiness and success in whatever you do. Here's to "Darkest Days" gone past.

Sincerely,

Will Z.

IV

Poems & Lyrics

Forward to My Unborn

We stared at the stars from in her closed room
Your mother's sweet music you hear in your womb
But my heart, it won't heal as your eyes cannot see
Your hands can't touch or reach for your daddy
In the beat of my heart, I'd have taken your place
Bring rain, watch her pain be erased
Through woods you won't walk
With eyes that won't see
In my heart, you'll always be a part of me

No beauty of winter or sound of the rain
Will you ever feel as we kept you from pain
From the world outside but you'll always be
A part in our hearts and we'll always be three

Visions of us walking paths laden in snow
We'll never walk, nor talk and I won't watch you grow
As 1 was 2 and 2 then made 3
And your shadow will always walk right behind me

A world less 1 soul, our hearts left to bleed
One wide-open mouth we won't ever feed
Memories turn gray but I won't ever let go
And if you can hear, we still love you so

William D. Zimmerman

The Dead Still Dream (Unfinished)

Innocence dies
A mother's tears turn into snow
So sad, she cries
For a soul whose name she'll never know

With elderly eyes
A woman catches butterflies from bed
How soon, my demise?
For my love shall return then

I still call out to you
(I still cry)
I'm still right beside you
(Why'd I die?)
I still am near you
(You feel my scream)
I still can hear you
And I still dream

I still call out to you
(Still I need)
I'm still right beside you
(Still I bleed)
And like an ever, an ever-flowing stream
I still am growing
(And I still dream)

The Dead Still Dream

* This song was never really finished but I included some of the
lyrics because I liked them and I wanted to share. While I was
thinking about the baby and the abortion, I was also thinking

about the loss of my grandma who died in 1997. There is one over-riding theme throughout these lyrics.

In the Baha'i faith, it's believed that the spiritual progress of a person's time on earth is continued in the afterlife. It's also believed that Heaven and Hell are more of a psychological reflection rather than a physical location. So I sort of took that idea, maybe exaggerated it a bit and suggested that the people who we loved and lost still have feelings, thoughts and dreams etc.

When my grandma passed away, I was struck by a couple of things that had occurred when she was in the nursing home. At one point she looked like she was grabbing at things in mid-air. When someone in the room asked what she was doing, she replied with "I'm catching the butterflies." Another time she asked my aunt, "When's Dad coming back?" "Mom, Dad's been dead for years," my aunt said. My grandma replied with "No." "He was here earlier and said he'd be coming back." Whether it was the medication or the fact that she was that close to next life, who are we to say that what she saw wasn't true?

William D. Zimmerman

Halo of Snowflakes

I am a child of the snow
I came to you when cold winds blew
As snowflakes fallen on the ground
I was the "I Love You" you never knew

The tears inside the hand of God
Will fall to earth below
And provide this one who's winter born
With a halo made of snow

I was a child of the snow
And I will leave as cold winds blow
You'll come to know me through your grief
And carry me where you will go

A Safe Place Away

And here I will stay
A safe place away
Where the winds never change

And here I will fade
With the clowns on parade
Where the guilty are sane

And here I'll remain
Where the sun does refrain
Where there's nothing to lose......... and nothing to gain

So here I will stay
And here I will play
And here I will pray

A safe place away

William D. Zimmerman

"Daddy, ...No!"

Though tears may fall down to the ground below
Still I hear you crying, "Can you hear me?...Daddy, No!"

Still I hear you pleading
And I hear you bleeding

Screaming,
Dreaming, "Daddy,...No!"

And when I fall or lose my way,
Still I can hear you say……..

Screaming
Pleading
Crying

"Daddy, No!"

Father, Forgive Yourself

Father, please forgive yourself, for you knew not what you'd
    done
You did the best you could and showed love through all your
    actions

Father, please forgive yourself, for I'm in a much safer place
No hate, nor pain or violence or sense of time and space

Father, please forgive yourself, it's not worth the burden you
    bare
While I'm here, I'm always near and while you're not always
    aware

Father, please forgive yourself, for the weight of the world you
    hold
And step outside into the winds, those winds that once blew
    cold

William D. Zimmerman

Half Past My Darkest Hour

Blessed be he who sleeps
For he shall rest some more
 Blessed be the writer, gifted
Of a never-written score
 Blessed be he who feels the chill
Of solitude's breeze
 And he who dwells, inside his hell
Never walking between the trees

Blessed be he who mourns a
Love he never had
 And blessed be the soul left torn
Found comfort being sad
 Blessed be he who shuns
The sun's unwelcome rays
 And reasons why, the seasons die
He dwells and sings its praise

Blessed be the sorrow-filled & their tomorrow filled with pain
For they did choose the less-traveled path
And caused the snow and rain

*I wrote this one at a real low point. I had developed a comfort zone and had gotten so used to feeling as bad as I was. That's basically what this is about. It's not that it's not okay to feel sad or depressed once in a while, but I had gotten so used to it that it felt strange to feel happy or hopeful.

Closing the Casket

I close the casket on the life I knew
And on the life that never grew

I close the casket on all I've known
And begin anew as I have grown

I close the casket on all my sins
And all regrets and "What-could-have-beens"

I close the casket and say goodbye
To the time when I did not try

And herein is my eulogy
For the person that I used to be

I close the casket on this life I made
And with this end....begins a new decade

William D. Zimmerman

Snowdrift

And like the snowflakes, each one in a million
You drifted,
As quickly as you came

The Avant-Guardian Angel

By the warmth of the ghostly touch on my hand......

And love knows no shape or color
And love-it holds no frame
And love needs no public display
Though love bleeds no shame

And love needs no museum
And love-it needs no "show"
For the Avant-Guardian Angel
Who fell those years ago

William D. Zimmerman

The Bleeding Tree

For every branch that's broken
And every leaf that falls
A story's told of those who set one free

For every limb that's pruned
And each frost-bitten root
A story's told beneath the bleeding tree

And for all the snow-glazed leaves
And for everyone who grieves
A story's written path to lead one free

And for every seed that's planted
And a life taken for granted

A story lives beneath the bleeding tree

Come Down from the Heavens

Come down from the heavens
My angel, my dear
The world is alight
As long as you're here

Come down from the heavens
My angel, my sweet
I'll worship the ground
That is graced by your feet

Come down from the heavens
My angel, my grace
I've dreamt of the glow
From the look on your face

I'm singing aloud
To the heavens above
I'll love you forever
My angel, my love

William D. Zimmerman

Should the World Crumble Beneath Us

Should the earth crumble beneath us
While we walk on sacred ground
While the rain pulsates outside this room
Our hearts the only sound

Should the heavens fall around us
Should the world just fall apart
I would treasure every moment
Of the beating of your heart

And should our castle crumble
And should you lose your crown
And should we be, lost at sea
With you, at least I'm found

Should the dreams you're wearing
Start tearing at the seams
Should you cast their ashes
To the flowing crimson streams

And may your fears cease to exist
And may your tears subside
And when you're lost along this shore
May I be your only guide

May angels fall from heaven
Taking guard by your side
Taking notes from your grace
Should they look inside your eyes

May I draw you down the moon...
May I part the heavens above you
May I hold steadfast inside your eyes
For I will always love you

Untitled

At least you won't know anger
At least you won't know depression
At least you won't know regret
As you were sent straight back to heaven

At least you won't know sadness
At least you won't know pain
At least you won't know the loss of love
For you sit above the rain

At least you can know love
At least you can forgive
But if only you had one chance
At least you could have lived

William D. Zimmerman

The Prayer

I am no one without you
And I am nothing without you
And I'll go nowhere without you
And I'll be no one without you

And I will sing no more
And I will pray no more
And I will say no more
If I am no more, without you

I am boundless within you
And I am fearless within you
And I am searching within you
And I am reaching toward you

Acts of Faith

Act I: Resignation

I know not why you've brought me here
With ropes of regret and bound by fear

It would take an act of God for me to feel "alive."

You held my hand and then let go
And so I fell to Hell below

A forgotten grace and loss of faith….a seemingly endless dive

In a grand resign

I just know…

That the only way is down

William D. Zimmerman

Acts of Faith

Act II: Revelation

Before my face, it's been made clear
The reasons why you brought me here

And you've been with me the whole entire time

You wrote the words for my life's song
Now I'm *alive*, I sing along

An act of faith full of reason and rhyme

The underlying
The undying
The never-ending

Acts of Faith

Act III: Restoration

I repaint life in great detail
Your hand in mine, I will prevail

With all the paints and colors I can adorn

Now that I know your sacred name
I place my life inside your frame

And in this act of faith, I am reborn

Farewell

Goodbye Dearest Angel

It's time to let you go

You'll ride forever's wings

Our child of the snow

A Vow in the Snow

Now, I understand...

These drops of blood inside my hand

IV
Afterword

"LIKE LESS OF A DORK"

During the summer of 2001 I went to see the band Stabbing Westward perform at a club called The Galaxy in St. Louis. I had been looking forward to this show for several weeks and I knew that the club would be packed. I also knew that after the show the tour bus would have a crowd around it; a crowd of fans waiting to talk to the band or to hopefully get autographs. Nevertheless, I was determined to let the members of the band know how important the "Darkest Days" and self-titled albums were to me. There's just something about those albums that, I believe, lets the listener know that it's not unusual to feel alone, complacent, depressed or to have ups and downs at times. They were one of those bands that made you feel "not so alone." I've always believed it's important to let someone know that their work was appreciated or even inspirational, but I knew the band would be mobbed with fans. So I decided to explain my feelings in a simple letter.

On the day of the concert I composed a half-page letter during a break at work. I explained my appreciation for their music, most specifically the two aforementioned CDs. I wrote how those albums really reminded me not so much of "dark days" per se, but rather how I had grown from what was perhaps the darkest time of my life. I mentioned the abortion and thanked them for their small part in getting me through those days. I handed the letter to their bass player, Jim before the concert. I also mentioned the letter to their lead vocalist, Christopher.

After the concert, I stood outside with the expected crowd of fans near the tour bus. I thought to myself, "I'm no more important than any of these people. I wonder if they even read my letter." Christopher walked out of the club with a girl both to his left and right sides, looked directly at me and said, "You wrote that letter." "Yeah," I said. "That was me." He thanked me for the letter and said that he appreciated hearing from fans that understood or "got" something from his music. He said, "It makes me feel like less of a dork." That would be the last tour Stabbing Westward would do before they broke up. So I was happy I got my point across and let them know I appreciated something they did.

That's really one of the many main purposes of life, isn't it? At least it should be. That is, to make sure everyone we meet is not taken for granted and that they know something they did or said is appreciated. There's a point to every relationship whether you meet someone on the street for a moment or if someone stands by your side during your entire life.

What's the point of this story in relation to this book? Perhaps it's that regardless of what experiences we go through as individuals be it good, bad or whatever; we can feel good that we left no relationship incomplete. More importantly, we can have the opportunity to let someone else know that they are appreciated or that they have had a positive effect on us.

I guess I just would like someone to feel, after reading this book, as though they too are "less of a dork."

** ** **

A SEASON DIES AND A NEW ONE ARRIVES

An odd feeling washes over me when I realize that I'm nearly done with this book. In one sense it feels like I'm *losing* a part of me. I suppose you could say that it feels as though a part of me is being laid to rest though not in an abrupt sense as in an abortion. It's more like a peaceful memorial service. But while I feel the passing of this chapter of my life, I also feel as though I'm giving birth to a new chapter.

I think that there has been a part of me that felt by nurturing this project, this labor of love, that I was nurturing the memory of our child. At times it didn't really feel as though the important thing was necessarily the *completion* of the book but rather the *process* or *progress* of it sort of in the way one would nurture a real relationship. That is, when someone is involved in a relationship, the main "objective" is not to "complete" it per se, but rather to make sure the relationship doesn't stay stagnant. However, in relationships between two individuals, if one does end, it's best to make certain it's not left incomplete. After all, hindsight is 20/20 and the worst of feelings are the dreadful "what-could-have-beens" or regrets.

Maybe I just didn't want to let go. After all, if we can't have someone we love around, who wants to let go of a memory even if what is left is not a direct remnant. I think that's part of the reason why this took what seems like forever and a day to complete.

Toward the end of writing this book, my mind was telling me, for the majority of the time that I pretty much had documented all that I wanted to say. Then there was another part of me that felt like I should tell more, like there was something being left out although I couldn't quite figure out what it was. Maybe it was just the feeling of that "missing piece" that my angel was supposed to occupy. Eventually, I just decided to let it be, so to speak. I sort of figured that I had finally arrived at a place of peace with regard to the abortion. I accepted the fact that, in life, there are sometimes questions that remain unanswered.

So, over the course of the last ten years, mainly the beginning and ending of writing this book, I have noticed two very distinct ….."struggles," shall we say. The first struggle, of course, was the actual emotional and psychological survival after the abortion. The second was the *documentation* of that struggle and the growth that eventually came. I not only had to overcome it emotionally, but I also had to battle my self-doubt over writing this book and the fear of its release; a fear that was taking on my conviction that this book was *supposed* to happen.

Transitions are frequently awkward or uncomfortable, even if the end result is positive or uplifting. When we, as people get used to a situation, especially for a span of months or years, then not having to deal with that situation can be somewhat uncomfortable. As strange as that sounds, that's often the case. A perfect example of that is the fact that this book sometimes remained on the shelf for a number of months at a time.

PROVING TO MYSELF

I can recall being a student at the university studying in the library for any one of my art history exams. I remember sitting in one of the many cubicles and looking beyond the scratched up surfaces of the solid wood desks and staring in amazement at the large collection of Masters theses and PhD dissertations. The fact that thousands of hours of discipline went into completing those bodies of work was awe-inspiring to me. The discipline it took to write those theses and dissertations seemed larger than life. Likewise, I have always had a strong admiration for authors who completed books.

As an art history major, I had become very familiar with the procrastination and the dread that came with writing research papers during my five years in college. However, I had also known the satisfaction of completing a paper after a few weeks of study

I don't think I ever *really* believed that I could write an entire book though. Or maybe at least part of me didn't believe this. That's another reason why I decided to make a book out of my story-to prove myself wrong. I not only wanted to succeed in healing. I also wanted to succeed in publishing a work that I previously didn't quite think that I could complete.

Nevertheless, while in one sense it feels like I'm losing a part of myself by closing this chapter of my life, I also have an immense feeling of joy knowing that this book is nearly done. In other words, I feel as though I'm giving birth to a new chapter in my life. This is, in fact, the feeling that overrides all of the others.

Most importantly though, is the possibility that this book could land in the hands of someone who could gain something positive from reading about my experiences. I believe that there are probably several reasons why I lived through those "darkest days." This book serves to document my highs and lows as well as my depression and revelation. With that in mind, if this book can help a person gain a new perspective or help them to open a new chapter in their life, then all of the hundreds and hundreds of hours which I have devoted to writing this have not been in vain.

Each sentence put a thought in the past, yet each sentence brought me closer to another stage in my life. It's nice that this book has now been completed. So once again, one chapter closes and a new one begins.

One season dies as a new one arrives.

** ** **

THE TREE OF LIFE: PART II

It was a morning in early September of 2004 when I awoke unusually early. I had a strange craving for Apple Jacks cereal. I put on my socks and shoes, got into my truck, adjusted my rear-view mirror and drove to the grocery store 3 blocks away. As though it were second nature, I turned on the radio for the company of whichever station I felt like befriending at the time.

The funny thing is that I don't recall tuning the radio to the Christian station at any time during the evening prior. Nevertheless, what I immediately heard the man on the radio say struck a nerve with me. He said, "Sometimes God prunes the smaller branches in order for the larger branches to grow and bear fruit." My ears were glued to the radio as I listened to him talk. I must have sat in my truck in the grocery store parking lot for at least ten to fifteen minutes listening to this program. Why was I listening to this? Was *I* supposed to hear it? I don't normally listen to the religious radio programs. What did it mean to me? Maybe it was coincidence that I heard this program. Then again, it couldn't be. I don't believe in coincidence.

Nevertheless, the message paralleled different things that were going on in my life at the time. I say this because I was single, I had been feeling alone and I had been without a job for a few months.

As soon as I returned to my apartment, I wrote that very poignant message on the dry erase board that hung on my refrigerator.

*"Sometimes God prunes the smaller branches in order
for the larger branches to grow and bear fruit."*

No two trees are the same and having such a huge fruit-bearing branch pruned, such as in the case of an abortion, alters the tree's life forever.

In the Introduction I spoke a bit about the references to trees as in the "tree of life," and the "family tree." I paralleled these references to the broken Christmas tree sticker in my rear-view mirror of my truck. There's that old question, "If a tree falls in the forest and there's no one around to hear it, does it make a sound?" The answer is "Of course it does." We can use that illustration when we lose a child to abortion. The "sound" resonates far beyond the forest where the "tree" fell and long after it fell. It resonates in the hearts of those men and women who have ever lost a child or for that matter, anyone they loved dearly. It is especially tricky for men because the sounds are more often silenced by society or even by some men, themselves. While men are often taught by society to be strong and to show less emotion, there aren't many options of discourse or places for men to go so that they don't feel quite so alone. Thankfully, there are at least a handful of organizations on the internet and elsewhere for men who've lost children to abortion. Certainly there are more that exist now than when I started this book.

** ** **

I had a fortune cookie once with a fortune that said, "Life is a comedy for those who think and a tragedy for those who feel." Out of the hundreds, or perhaps more likely, thousands of fortune cookies I have eaten over the years, that fortune remains to be one of the very few that I recall.

Several years ago, I would likely have been more inclined to view life as a tragedy, especially after the abortion. As I've grown older I tend to view life as more of a combination of both comedy and tragedy. It's healthy to feel hurt, anger and depression at times. However, it's not only healthy but rather, *necessary* to also feel hope, love and laughter. At the same time, one should keep a healthy balance of "thinking" and "feeling." If you always let your heart lead your head, the end result can be naivety. If, however, you find that your heart always follows your head, then you're thinking too much and not feeling enough.

One thing that I've at least given myself credit for even in the middle of the rough times is that I've always been in tune with my emotions and I've always been aware of my behaviors. Maybe it's the artist in me.

The pain of enduring the many emotions I've had after losing a child to abortion has become easier to manage as time has progressed. I am at peace with the situation now. I am at peace with the old feelings of regret and self-hatred that I once had. I have since found forgiveness not only for Anne, but for myself as well.

My hindsight is now 20/20 and I'm satisfied with the perspective I have regarding my growth since those first thoughts and emotions surrounding the abortion. However, that growth didn't come without a lot of growing pains.

** ** **

Writing this book has been extremely therapeutic. In fact, writing it has proved to be some of the most effective therapy that I have had. However, it's not been all of it. I use the illustration of a musician and producer who are in the studio creating an album. It's always helpful to have the ears of an extra person to assist in the mixing of tracks, effects and the appropriate levels of volume. A producer might help an artist emphasize their strengths and tune their weaknesses.

Often the perspective of another person can help make one aware of thoughts and feelings they hadn't been previously aware of. This can help the process of healing a great deal. Sometimes it's a friend. However, I think that for some friends the topic of abortion can often be an uncomfortable discussion; one that all too often ends with the friend suggesting that you should "get over it" or that you should "move on."

Other times therapy can be with a parent or perhaps more effectively, a professional therapist. I have been fortunate enough to work with a couple of therapists who I feel more comfortable calling "emotional production assistants." That's not to suggest that they help you produce new emotions but rather they help you sort out what's already inside of you. I've noticed three steps in the process of healing. The first is awareness, the second is sorting out or making sense of a situation and the third is what to do in working toward healing.

There's no shame in bluntly honest human emotions. Society tends to favor holding emotions inside. This is especially the case for men which, of course, is B.S.

ADVICE

While I wasn't sure how to segue into this, I wanted to include a section in this portion of the book containing some items of advice and perhaps some examples of things that I've done or learned. These particular things have either directly helped in the healing process or just simply made me feel better about myself along the way. You can take them or leave them but they worked for me and in some cases helped others in the process.

As I said in the Foreword, I don't profess to be an expert or celebrity or anything like that. I'm just a relatively simple person who's passing on the knowledge and experiences that I have received.

- *__Allow__*
  It may sound generic but here's the thing. First and foremost, you need to allow yourself the opportunity to cry, scream or simply *feel* whatever comes your way. However, this should definitely be used in conjunction with the next suggestion. Additionally, you will need to allow yourself to not only forgive yourself, but also your partner who also likely experienced emotions such as sadness, anger, regret or depression. If nothing else, finding forgiveness for your partner could be beneficial to you as it may help you to arrive at a place of peace within yourself.

- *__Write__*
  Write whatever you are thinking or feeling. Write to survive if you need to. That's what I did. It could keep you from going insane. Sometimes there are no more powerful weapons to battle inner demons than a journal and a pen. Simply put, some of the best therapy you can buy costs less than a couple of dollars at the store.

This will allow you to purge the good, the bad and the ugly thoughts that cloud your head. It will allow you to document and begin making sense of things. One thing I experienced is that I had feelings and emotions that really hadn't manifested until I stopped *thinking* and started *writing*. You don't have to publish. However, if you feel that you have a story worth publishing, please share it, especially if you're a man.

Here's one exercise you can try if you're having trouble exorcising your inner demons: On a piece of paper in your notebook write about a half-dozen words, for example, "grief," "emotion," "faith," "bereavement," "love" and "memory." Around each of those words write the first words that come to mind even if they don't necessarily mean something in direct reference to the word you draw from. As a matter of fact, you might be able to do one word on each page. It's an old English class exercise but it really helps to ignite the thought process. You might also consider doing other forms of artistic expression such as poetry or even music. You'll know that you're on the path to healing when you feel you are ready to share your thoughts and experiences.

- ***Talk to Someone***
  While the act of writing your thoughts down is often a cathartic experience and may be the best thing you can do for yourself, it's not one hundred percent of the solution. You need to speak to another human being, especially if you've experienced a loss like an abortion. It can be a friend, relative, therapist or whomever; someone you can trust. An extra ear to listen and help you work through your sadness can be one of the most beneficial things. One thing to keep in mind, though, the advice of a trusted friend or relative might not always

be welcome. Stick with those people who aren't going to always tell you what you *want* to hear. Rather, it's more beneficial to be around people who will tell you what you *need* to hear. Furthermore, completely ignore people who dismiss your pain when they tell you to "just get over it." Remember that your emotions and your healing aren't necessarily bound by the chains of time.

- ### *Participate in online blogs or email groups*
  If you have suffered the loss of your child to abortion, there are a few places on the internet you might find. If you are a man, almost all of the places you can turn to are on the internet. You might have a harder time locating groups specifically for men but there are more out there now than when I started this book. I'm including some of the ones I've found in the back of this book in the Resources section.

- ### *Read*
  Read articles in magazines, on the internet or books. The more you read and are informed about other men and women who have had similar experiences, the less likely to feel alone you will be. This one could also go hand in hand with the aforementioned suggestion. You can read blogs and join email lists but you won't truly benefit from them unless you participate. I feel the same about reading and the previously mentioned journal writing.

- ### *Volunteer*
  Find local charity groups or organizations that need volunteers. Volunteer for a hospital or other medical facility. One of the most gratifying things that I've found is providing service to someone in need. You

also don't have to just volunteer on holidays. It's like going to church only on Sundays or holidays. You can also provide donations for children, perhaps on the anniversary of your loss. You could use my idea of donating stuffed animals to local police departments. Just call your local police offices and see what they would like and if they could accept donations. Again, this is not the only solution for healing but it should definitely make you feel better about yourself.

In my case, as I've grown older, I've found meaning within faith and bringing joy to others. The latter has come in different forms. On occasions, it's a small donation of stuffed animals to police departments. When officers are called to homes where a domestic violence call came from, stuffed animals are often given to the children in effort to provide comfort for an obviously scary situation.

I have also ventured into the field of stand-up comedy. It felt good to put myself in a position where I had to make quick decisions without *thinking*. I've always felt that it was a gift to be able to make someone laugh, especially a complete stranger. The ability to make another person laugh is a simple gift but one that should never be taken for granted. As strange as it may seem, I think that it is considerably easier to make people laugh when there are two hundred people in the audience as opposed to ten people.

Moreover, there is a purpose to every individual relationship in life whether it is in making someone smile for a moment or a life-long commitment.

** ** **

In the Introduction I referred to moments or memories in my life as "snapshots."

However, I sometimes prefer to view life as one large painting with either an old wood or glossy frame. Each thread of the canvas represents a relationship and like most relationships, many threads cross one another. Depending on the durability or quality of the thread, the carelessness of the artist or vandalism by a "viewer," the threads can possibly break. In sort of the same way if we, the "artists" break off a relationship or a thread in the canvas, we must choose to start from scratch or repair the thread as best as possible though it will never be *just* like the original. Hopefully the thread will be just as strong as or perhaps stronger than it was before.

Likewise, healing after the loss of a child to abortion is in many ways like the restoration of a priceless painting. It can be a painstaking process. Often the process involves deframing the canvas and gently cleaning off the dust and mildew. The final step is putting the frame back on the canvas.

Vincent Van Gogh never sold a painting until after his death. But perhaps much in the way people didn't fully appreciate Van Gogh until after his death, so do we as humans often not realize what we have been given until those things are no longer there.

My angel is no longer here. I have but a drawing, and the contents of this book-a document of who I was and who I've become.

** ** **

My friend Tom of the band Arcanta once said to me, "I think the most we can do as people is inspire one another so if something I've done has touched you then my life and work have not been in vain."

Someone else once said that there's a difference in *living* and being *alive.*

I try hard to live with these two principles in the foreground of my mind. You know what keeps me going every day when I wake up? It really boils down to three simple things: faith, love and hope, but mainly hope. I learned a long time ago that if you don't have even a small sense of hope or a sense of *looking forward* you're only *living* and not being *alive*.

I hope today will be better than yesterday. I hope something I say or do will help someone in a positive way-whether it is something as simple as a compliment or something more like a labor of love such as this book. These days I hope for a lot of things. Most of all, I hope the hands that receive a copy of this book reach out and help someone else.

This is my story and I truly hope you've gained something from it.

** ** **

"and then i prevail again, again
as all these memories pass again
i look ahead to the new day again
please no more dark days, dark days

again, again

and from the top of the mountain
i stare down on new flowers
and go straight into a new day"

Lycia – "These Memories Pass"

** ** **

UPDATE: 2007

As I've said before, a new season begins as an old one dies.

And as it is so often the case, things sometimes happen when and where you least expect them to.

On New Years Day, 2005, I met the woman who was to become the love of my life. I would realize this only a mere 3 weeks later. I know that sounds crazy but it's true. Though the internet was a place that I had long since sworn off as a location to meet "the one," that's exactly where I met her. While our relationship has had more than its share of roller coasters, curveballs and storms, there's also been a tremendous amount of joy too.

She gave to me the opportunity to have a positive effect on the lives of three wonderful young men who I consider to be like my own. Then on April 18, 2006, she gave birth to a son of our own. Ian Michael Zimmerman was born 3 weeks early at 12:20 AM.

When I started this book, I felt the weight of my own grief, bereavement, regret, guilt and a huge empty hole in my heart. Today that hole has been filled and I now feel a completeness the likes of which I have never known. Not only do I have the person that I have always wanted to share my life with, but I've also got four awesome young men roaming around the house.

I have a different vehicle now but hopefully that Christmas tree sticker is still on the rear-view mirror of the pick-up truck for whoever the driver is now.

Some people measure their success in terms of finances or their career. As I sit here and type these last words, with Ian in playing with his cars, his brothers in their rooms or watching movies and my wife Christy at my side, I look around and realize: Life has come full circle and I've succeeded.

** ** **

In Conclusion

I'm standing in the rooftop garden sanctuary of the hospital I work at. The rain has ceased but the wooden walkway and short stone wall is still wet from the rain. Between the sunset on the horizon and the fence that protects this garden are several meandering bicycle paths and side streets. On those paths and streets are a number of individuals who've got one simple goal for the moment-to get to their destination.

A number of thoughts and emotions overwhelm me simultaneously as I look upon those people on the paths and streets. These days, however, floods of thoughts and emotions don't arrive like an unwelcome snowstorm or tornado as they once did. Rather, they come at me like a mild autumn breeze-the kind I don't mind standing in for a while.

I think about the days when my goal was traveling to where I needed to go during the course of the last ten years of my life. Whether it was traveling to Kansas or coming back home; whether it was finishing one section of this book or the entire book itself, I'm able to look into the rear-view mirror with perfect 20/20 vision.

I also think about the place I work at and the things I see almost daily that make me grateful for the people in my life and the relationships that I have with those people. Those relationships are the real blessings. I consider the fact that this is a place where families don't always go home happy and where patients sometimes don't go home. I think of all of the hopes and dreams that are lost here as well as those that are saved. I also think of those hopes and dreams held by the people I see traveling on the paths and streets below.

It's been years since the bad dreams stopped and the waves of depression, regret, anger and guilt have washed up on the shores of time. Though I never would have imagined a decade ago that I'd be saying this, those "Darkest Days" were in some ways a curse. However, in other ways they were a blessing.

As I stand near the edge of this building, I'm reminded of the extremes that my life has seen over the past decade. I have traveled to Hell and back again. I have lived through nights when I didn't want to wake up the next morning. I have also been incredibly blessed, especially in the past few years.

So whether it's in this garden, in my basement, under the covers or in the woods during winter, I'm reminded of these things:

Life and relationships should never be taken for granted. Never leave a relationship incomplete. Learning to forgive one's self is a process and takes time. It's important to lead an inherently selfless life and the most noble of pursuits is that which nurtures and improves the lives of children. It's important to take time out of the day and remind one's self of the blessings in life.

As I turn to go back inside, one last thought remains in my mind. It's really the only unanswered question left. Yet, it's the most important question. Can this document of my experience help even one other individual?

One person
Between the edge of this rooftop sanctuary
And through the horizon ahead
And beyond
Whether in a car, a bedroom or a waiting room.........

I truly hope so.

"Life can only be understood backwards,

but it must be lived forward."

- Soren Kierkegaard

Addendum

WHY DID IT TAKE SO LONG?

Parts of this book were written sporadically over the past ten years. As I said before though, I didn't start writing this until about eighteen months after the abortion took place.

I think that there are two fundamental reasons why this project took so long for me to complete. The first reason has to do with the nature of the situation. There was the rawness of my thoughts and emotions during the first couple of years after the abortion. Then there was the fact that I had to relive the experience of the loss and the emotions that surrounded it each time I wrote as well as each time I did a revision. Being so close to an extreme situation, one's viewpoint is often too muddy as mine was. At times I felt I was only able to handle taking "baby steps" in my writing. I couldn't realize how the abortion affected me or who I would become until time had allowed me to process it and heal. I had to get a safe distance away from the situation to achieve a healthy and reasonably objective viewpoint.

Sometimes I would let this project sit on the shelf for weeks or months at a time. I would attend to it when the tide of inspiration would wash over me and I could wash some of the dirt away. That's the thing about dealing with the gravity of a situation like an abortion or losing a child. You can recall your experiences as a result of it many times vividly as though the situation occurred only yesterday.

The second reason why this book took so long is perhaps fear. Within that resides the fear of success as well the fear of failure. My many "what-ifs" not only came as a result of the abortion. They also came in the form of questions such as "What if this book *actually* succeeds in helping a significant number of people?" Helping someone else through a traumatic experience can be scary in and of itself when you, yourself are dealing with a traumatic situation as well. For a while, I didn't feel that I deserved the rewarding feeling of knowing that I assisted someone else through a difficult time. After all, for at least the first couple of years after the abortion, I felt that because of my responsibility, I deserved the heartache that I was suffering.

I was also sensitive to the fear of failure as well. I thought, "What if this book flops and fails to reach the people who could possibly need it?" After all, I felt I had committed the biggest failure of all. As you'll read, that was my feeling of failing to attempt to defend our baby's life.

One of the biggest fears that I encountered while writing this book was the thought, "What am I going to do when I'm done with this book?" "What will I do when I *have* to let go?" "Am I going to be as inspired again and if so, is it going to take a tragedy to inspire me?"

I have sometimes wondered if the more time I allowed to pass before this book reaches publication, the less valid or "fresh" it would be or the less likely to be published it might become. However, grief is not only intimate and immediate, it's timeless and universal. Additionally, grief does not discriminate against race, religion, gender or age. The same could be said about hope. In her book, Unreliable *Truth: On Memoir and Memory*, Maureen Murdock says the following:

"Memoir trades on the universality of memories, reflecting the dreams, desires, and feelings we all share. Regardless of whether the specific facts of your life are different from mine, we can both relate to the…..sense of wonder watching the first snowfall of the season, the sense of adventure in traveling to a new land or the grief and disbelief involving the death of a loved one. The facts are individual but the feelings are universal."

With thoughts similar to Murdock's in mind, I knew that this book would arrive when it was *supposed* to. I am convinced that this book exists for a greater purpose than just to serve as a document of my experience. I know that it's supposed to help people. At times, I think that realization, while very humbling, also can be a bit scary. Yet there has been something driving me for he last few years to finish this book. I don't know whether it's been God, my angel or what. Nevertheless, something wouldn't let me quit.

There were times during the writing of this book when I wanted to smile, cry or even walk outside with my hands held high and pull the heavens down to the ground.

There were times when I wanted to grab God by the shirt collar and ask him "Why?"

Basically, I wanted to capture the joy and the pain; the hurt and the heartache. I wanted to tap into those universal emotions that every human being faces even though the specifics of our situations may differ greatly at times.

** ** **

AUDIENCE AND NICHE

Since the vision for this project turned from a journal into a book which consumers might pick up, I've taken into consideration the different types of people who might find it online or in a book store. To say that this book is intended exclusively for men to read is a mistake.

I think anyone who wants to read a first-hand account of a man's experience with abortion may gain a new perspective from this book as well. Additionally, I would like this book to be meaningful to people in their teens as well as those in their later years of life. Sadness, happiness and triumph over life's challenges are universal experiences and should not be thought to be exclusive to either gender or to those of any particular age group.

So, the universality of human emotions has been the primary reason why I chose to structure this book the way I did. Likewise, I would like readers of this book to be able to pick it up and either read a few pages of the Letters section or glance through the Poems section and be inspired.

I also hope this book will help the family members and friends of those who have dealt with the loss of a child through abortion. I hope it will help provide a window into the range of emotions their loved-ones could be dealing with. What better way for someone to attempt to assist another person through a painful journey than to try and place their feet into the shoes of the person they care about? It should be mentioned though, that there will be times when you won't be able to help the person who is directly dealing with the loss. Sometimes the best thing or the *only* thing you can do is to simply be there when that person needs you and offer to be along for the ride.

Given the fact that I may very well have a decent niche to market this book to, in the same breath of air, I also have to ask myself the question; why take this book into the court of public opinion? Why throw my work into the faces of those who might scrutinize my language or criticize my perspective? Why publicize such private thoughts and feelings? I have been told on numerous occasions by acquaintances that I was "brave" to disclose such painful experiences to the public.

I came to the conclusion that any potential criticism, complaints, etc. that could arrive as a result should this composition actually reach the publishing stage would be far outweighed by my motives and intentions in writing this.

About the Author

William Zimmerman was born in 1974 and spent most of his life in Edwardsville, Illinois and St. Louis, Missouri. In 1997 he graduated from Southern Illinois University at Edwardsville with a Bachelor's Degree in Art history. Currently he resides in southern Illinois with his wife Christy, son Ian and 3 step-sons: James, Seth and Hunter.

Will has been working on a collection of short stories that has yet to be titled. He is also pursuing a second Bachelor's Degree and certification in health information technology.

Recommended Reading

Below is a list of books that I either read along my journey of healing or just inspired me in one way or another

Fatherhood Aborted by Guy Condon & David Hazard, Tyndale House Publishers (May 11, 2001)

Swallowed by a Snake: The Gift of the Masculine Side of Healing by Thomas R. Golden, Golden Healing Publishing LLC; 2nd edition (November 2000)

Empty Cradle, Broken Heart: Surviving the Death of Your Baby by Deborah L. Davis, Fulcrum Publishing; Revised & enlarged edition (1996)

Writing to Heal the Soul: Transforming Grief and Loss through Writing by Susan Zimmerman, Three Rivers Press (February 12, 2002)

Finding Hope When a Child Dies by Sukie Miller, Fireside; 1st edition (August 15, 2002)

Unspeakable Losses: Healing from Miscarriage, Abortion, and Other Pregnancy Loss by Kim Kluger-Bell, Quill (2000)

When Hello Means Goodbye: A Guide for Parents Whose Child Dies before Birth, At Birth or Shortly After Birth

by Pat Schwiebert, RN and Paul Kirk, MD, *Perinatal Loss* (2001)

With Pen in Hand: The Healing Power of Writing by Henriette Anne Klauser, Da Capo Press (January 7, 2003)

Unreliable Truth: On Memoir and Memory by Maureen Murdock, Seal Press (2003)

The Courage to Write: How Writers Transcend Fear by Ralph Keyes, Holt Paperbacks (October 1, 2003)

Memoirs of the Soul: Writing Your Spiritual Autobiography by Nan Phifer, Walking Stick Press (December 1, 2001)

Escaping into the Open: The Art of Writing True by Elizabeth Berg, Perennial (2000)

On Writing: A Memoir of the Craft by Stephen King, Pocket Books (July 1, 2002)

Shimmering Images: A Handy Little Guide to Writing Memoir by Lisa Dale Norton, St. Martin's (2008)

Sleeping Beauty: Memorial Photography in America by Stanley B. Burns, M.D., Twinpalms / Twelvetree Press (1990)

> *This is a collection of photography from around the early 1900s. I can't say that the content itself was much of an inspiration to my book. However, the thing that I found most inspiring about this book was its blunt honesty in the documentation of post-death photography. Death is something that all too often is considered taboo in everyday conversations today. However, these were everyday people in those photographs in this book and all they wanted was a visual post-mortal memory.

Recommended Listening

Below is a list of albums that have helped carry me through the good and bad days during the years of writing this book and through the present day. Many of these releases are hard to find. However, I encourage you to search for and if possible, support these amazing artists.

Leaether Strip – Serenade for the Dead
This is, by far, my favorite instrumental album, really my favorite album of all time. While Claus Larsen of Leaether Strip has typically composed dance-oriented electronic music, this album was more symphonic and really like the soundtrack of a horror movie. If you can hunt this one down (good luck), put it in the CD player, turn off all the lights, light a few candles and let the album take your mind to a different world. You can likely locate this one on Ebay or from Amazon sellers.
http://www.myspace.com/leaetherstrip

Stabbing Westward – Darkest Days

Stabbing Westward – Stabbing Westward
These two above albums are very special to me. You might think that I like to listen to Darkest Days to put myself back in

that cluttered bedroom ten years ago. That's not the case. These to records remind me not of the darkness of the days back then, but rather the fact that I made it *through* them. The best track is "I Remember" off of the self-titled release.

Stay Frightened – Still
I could probably fill up a page and a half as to why I love this album. It was one of the first CDs I heard from the Palace of Worms label when I did some work for them years back. "Still" has never gotten old for me. My friend Conrad, otherwise known as Stay Frightened creates these ambient, fluid journeys and his lyrics and vocals are like something delicate flowing on top of the water. I am pretty sure the label has deleted this title. However, you might find some small European gothic/industrial mail order company that has a copy left.
http://www.myspace.com/stayfrightened

Lycia – Cold
If there ever was a soundtrack to remind me of a walk in the woods during winter, this would be it. Very dreamy and ethereal, Mike and Tara captured the dynamics of the winter landscape, the harshness of the cold and the beauty of the snow covered trees.
http://www.myspace.com/lycia

Human Drama – 14, 384 Days Later (Live)
Johnny's version of John Cale's "I Keep a Close Watch" is alone, worth hunting this CD down.

Human Drama – The World Inside
This is the one that features "Winter's Life" which I quoted in the Story. If you don't find even a small part of yourself in this CD, I'll buy it back from you. That is, again, if you can find this one. It's just tragic when the music industry fails to fully appreciate talent to the likes of this degree.

Human Drama – Songs of Betrayal
After my breakup with Anne, I listed to nothing but Human Drama for a bout one week straight. I remember singing along with the song "Blue" off this CD and just crying my eyes out. Even Johnny will probably tell you, listening to Human Drama exclusively for a week straight is probably not the smartest idea for getting through something, as their lyrics have always been very deep, emotional and dramatic. However, they are very honest and they often deal with feelings a lot of us would prefer not to face.

Some of Human Drama's releases are still available via their web site. However, for the more hard-to-find albums, you might try Ebay.
www.HumanDrama.net
http://www.myspace.com/humandramamusic
http://www.myspace.com/soundoftheblueheart
http://www.myspace.com/johnnyindovinamusic

Arcanta – The Eternal Return
Spiritual, multi-lingual and stirring. Thomas-Carlyle Ayres is the man behind the voice which is the main instrument here.
http://www.myspace.com/arcantamusic

Resources

This list is only a partial collection of the resources (mostly on the internet) where you can go to find help or just a wealth of information

www.webhealing.com
This web site is an invaluable resource run by Tom Golden, the author of Swallowed by a Snake. Whether you've suffered the loss of a child, parent, sibling etc., this site is a great way to connect with others who might be going through similar situations.

www.guysforlife.org
Great site run by my friend Kurt. Mostly deals with the subject of men who've dealt with abortion. Also check out his YouTube channel. It's http://www.youtube.com/user/guysforlifeorg#p/c/3328021C255D9047

www.fatherhoodforever.org
The site says it best when it says "Helping men find healing and hope after abortion."

www.lifeissues.org/men/
Pretty good site with several useful resources.

www.rachelsvineyard.org
This is a great idea though I've never tried it. They offer retreats in different areas of the USA for men and women who are struggling personally and spiritually after dealing with abortion.

www.noparh.org
This is the National Organization for Post Abortion Reconciliation and Healing. Not really sure what else to say but God Bless these people.

www.abortionrecovery.org
This site provides a large list of groups that provide healing services for men, as well as for other family members.

www.menandabortion.net
This is the Men and Abortion Network or MAN.

www.abortionrecoveryinternational.org
This site is just what the address says: The ARIN organization. There are TONS of great resources and links; way too many to mention for this small space.

www.silentnomoreawareness.org/
This site is definitely geared toward women and men. To quote the mission from the site, their goal "is that the emotional and physical pain of abortion will no longer be shrouded in secrecy and silence, but rather exposed and healed." There's also links for the campaign in a few different countries.

www.ramahinternational.org
This is another great web resource. This one is a ministry-site which has a wealth of information on it. There are resources, teaching materials, tons of articles and information for both men and women alike.

www.petalsandsage.com/
Neat website run by our friend Pam Richards; one of the nicest and most sincere individuals my wife and I have ever met.

Contact

You may contact the author, Will Z. directly at:
Dearestangelbook@yahoo.com

Please note that any email deemed insulting or abusive will
be immediately discarded without reply and if necessary,
reported as abuse and the address will be blocked.

Otherwise, you can find me here:

http://www.facebook.com/WillZ9919
http://www.myspace.com/inwinterbleeding

Or on my blogs:

http://inwinterbleeding.wordpress.com
http://abortionandmen.blogspot.com/